A Plain Understanding of The Red Dragon

By
Elijah Muhammad
(Messenger of Allah)

Published by
Secretarius MEMPS Publications
111 E Dunlap Ave, Ste 1-217
Phoenix, Arizona 85020-7802
Phone & Fax 602 466-7347
Email: secmemps@gmail.com
www.memps.com

ISBN10# 1-884855-82-2
EAN13# 978-1-884855-82-5

Printed in the United States of America

DEDICATION

To all the Believers and Followers
of
Elijah Muhammad,
Messenger of Allah,
without whom, we as fractions
would have no expectation
of ever
becoming whole.

~ ~ ~ ~ ~

The
Messenger
is a Sword
In A Man's Hand

~ Sayings of Elijah Muhammad, Vol. 3

TABLE OF CONTENT

THE POPE AND THE CATHOLIC CHURCH

Greetings to you. I am Elijah Muhammad, the preacher of freedom, justice and equality, to my people, the American so-called Negroes, who are not Negroes. They are a tribe and member of that great Asiatic Nation, by the name of Shabazz, from whom we came. We have been here in the Western Hemisphere, according to the word of Almighty God, Allah, to me, for 400 years; to Whom all praise is due, the Lord of the worlds. He is the One that all looked for to come and He has come, Almighty God in person.

We live in the day of a change of worlds; an old world going out and a new world coming in. We live in this change. We are happy and should be happy that Almighty God Allah has blessed us to see this day; wherein, the old evil world of sin and indecency is passing off the scene with all of her shows and work of evil and filth.   This world, as you and I now know, was the world of evil, given 6,000 years to try the righteous nation - the original nation of the earth - the black people. The white people were created and made for the purpose of ruling this people - the original nation - under a rule of evil, indecency, temptation and every kind of vice that is known to the science of man. The most evil and the most filthy temptation ever known to be displayed before man is now going on in this evil world which was [made] to live 6,000 years and do all the evil it possibly could.

These people are the murderers of God's prophets, the murderers of the righteous, the liars of the people, the deceivers of all the people, who have not the nature to be righteous, because there was none put in them. Murder was put into their hearts and mind when they were created. Their father put it into their hearts when they were made, and by nature, they are that . The proof is their work which they have done - murdering, lying and inviting people to evil and indecency. This is the ruling class of this world, called the white man's world.

This, you must now know today. These are the truths that were never brought out to the righteous people, who would turn from evil, who would turn from following after doing evil if they had only known the evil guide. Today, the man of sin is being revealed, as the Bible, II Thessalonians, teaches you, that there can be no judgement until that man of sin is revealed. The man of sin means one who is [made] of evil and that he has no good in him at all. By nature he's made that, which is what the Bible is referring to. This is not a person of good who has attracted or [contracted] evil or has been led by an evil one, but one that was made, by nature, of evil and one that, by nature, cannot help but to be evil - that is the white race.

The so-called American Negro who has no part whatsoever in this people, by nature, must be told the truth as it is written - "Ye shall know the truth..." - according to John saying these to be the words of Jesus, around the 37th verse of the 8th chapter of John. This truth now is being preached to you, my people. If it costs my life to tell you the truth, I must tell it. If it cost the life of all my followers, it must be told. A nation numbering between 22 and 25 million is more valuable than a few people who will sacrifice their lives for them, if that sacrifice is made by those who would love to see you free of your enemies, own some of this earth that you can call your own. Their names will be written in the book that will live forever, for a death that was sacrificed or a person who sacrificed his life for the good of a nation that will live forever and triumph over evil and trample it under their feet after it has been destroyed into ashes. This is an easy price to pay. It is a glorious price to pay; therefore, we, the Muslims, fear not our lives and care not for the consequences of telling the truth, preaching the truth, and trying to lead our people out of the hands and power of their enemies regardless to what it cost. We are the people who want to see our people live in peace, enjoying freedom, justice and equality as a civilized nation of the earth.

God Almighty has appeared among you and has missioned me, Elijah Muhammad, to preach the truth to you and warn you of the insinuations of the devil which will cause you to meet with total destruction with them. I want you to know for what reason the truth is really being preached to you. It is to save your own life from a destruction of a people with whom you have no part whatsoever in their destruction, except only you who are willing to ignore the truth and/or you who are absolutely in love with those who God is against and has prepared a mighty burning fire for them, a real hot fire has He prepared for this people.

He has no love for His enemies - the devil - who has killed His prophets, killed the righteous, deceived the righteous, and who has poisoned the Blackman's mind, here in America, against Him, against the truth, against righteousness and against good behavior and doing good. He has poisoned his mind towards death and has them following him to an open lake of fire, which God Almighty has prepared for this evil race of people. I say to you, as the Bible teaches you in Revelations, "Come out of her, come out of her, why will you die?" It teaches you to come out of her.

The Catholic church, Catholic religion, the priest, and the Pope of Rome are all after the Negroes in North America, the so-called Negroes - the Black people. They're inviting you to accept the Catholic religion; they're inviting you to associate and intermarry with them, while in the past, they did not want you in their church. The priest did not want you in his church to preach to. Now today, the whole of the Catholic people throughout the world and especially here in America has changed; whereas, the Pope of Rome is helping the government of America persuade the Negroes - the so-called Negroes - to accept the religion they call the Catholic religion.

Catholicism is the mother religion of Christianity and the Pope of Rome is recognized by the Christians to be the father of that religion, the father of the church and the intercessor between man and God. This is one of the most audacious, most deceitful and the worst religion on the earth to accept.

To accept a religion that has been declared to be the true religion of God, yet the base of that religion is against the principles and the wisdom of God himself: A belief in God, the father, belief in his son, as a helper to Him, belief in the Holy Ghost, as though the God is absolutely too weak to rule the Caucasian race; then has to prepare a son and make him to go and suffer death at the hands of the Caucasian people for Him to respect them again as his people.

They have never been the people of the True God, as Jesus said in the Bible, 8th chapter and 44th verse of John. He said their father was the devil. They are the children of the devil, their father was a liar, the truth doesn't abide in them and he was a murderer from the beginning. This was referring to the Caucasian or the white race of people. Jesus was sent to that people as a last prophet and he gave up on them as a nation or race of devils and said to them that his words of truth, which he preached, had no place in them, because there was no good in them; therefore, they could not accept him. He therefore paid with his life for trying to convert them to Islam, the true religion of God, which means entire submission to the Will of God. This is what Elijah Muhammad is asking you today, to submit to the Will of God. He's the Best Knower; rely on Him, take refuge in Him and He will protect you from the evil intentions of this race of devils, who has planned your destruction. They are leading you to total destruction and want you to die and be destroyed with them. They are absolutely killing you daily and beating you for even asking them for justice. This is the people who were made for the fire of hell. This is the people who God despises and hate that they were ever placed on the planet earth, but they were allowed to be put on it to try them at ruling; however, their time is now up and they are doing everything to try and stay by planing the total extermination of the Blackman. They are practicing it on you today - the so-called American Negroes.

I even heard talk that they are planning mass murder of the so-called Negroes, here in America, and plan to sterilize them to prevent them from continuing to produce a people like themselves. This is a plan that was made by Pharaoh, a plan that was made by Herod in the time of Jesus, just to keep these righteous people of God from multiplying on the earth. They plan the total destruction of them by killing off the males. This scientific nation right here, who has so much more knowledge of chemistry today and of drugs, plans the total destruction of you and me. They don't want the so-called America Negro, but they don't want him to return to his own people; yet, they will be forced one of these days to give them up.

There is no safety for you, only in the mercy of your God and my God, Allah Who has visited us in the person of Master Fard Muhammad, to Whom praise is due forever, for coming in the worst part of the planet earth and among the worst people. He suffered 3-1/2 years here. Even He Himself was prosecuted by this people. Twice I went to the jail house and got Him and brought Him out from this people for the truth that He brought to us and they ran Him out of Detroit. They then followed Him up to Chicago trying to give Him the worse [a hard time] for teaching us the truth. This truth is growing universally. It will change the whole entire world of the Blackman and the Blackman will be happy and will rejoin forever with this truth. It is gradually getting into the hearts of every Blackman on the earth.

You, my people, should unite. You should turn to your people, seek love, unity and justice in the midst of your own people. Seek equality with your people and stop trying to seek love, unity and equality with the devil, none of which has been put in him by nature. He was [made] as he is. He doesn't love himself; he doesn't love his own kind. They are at war with each other day and night.

They are killing each other day and night. How can they be an example of love and peace for the Blackman? How can they have a world of peace when they are always warring among themselves? How can they love the Blackman when they were [made] to be his enemy? I say, change your heart and your mind from looking forward to them for true guidance, looking forward to them leading you to the God of truth, the God of mercy, the God of righteous. They are not leading you to that in the judgement; they are leading you to hell with them.

I will stand on the top of Mount Everest and yell out if my voice and would do so all the way around the earth and prove to you that this religion, Christianity, was made for the purpose of enslaving black people and not to take them to heaven. It will not take you to Paradise; it will take you to hell, because the charges they made against God, accusing Him of being an adulterer by getting a child out of wedlock in Palestine 2,000 years ago, is the worst crime that they could have put against the Just and Righteous God, Who is not even married. He has no wife, but they are charging Him with such an act and you are believing it.

Surely there is a Son given and a government is put upon his shoulder. Surely that is right, but not for the Jews. It is for you the Black people. God has not created no paradise for the white race. When they were made, hell was set for them.

I say to you, my beloved, that you must be aware of the evil insinuations of this open enemy of righteousness and the haters of the so-called American Negroes, the murderers, lynchers and burners of our people, who now want to fool them by pretending they want to be friendly with them. This is like a cat toying with a mouse, but intend to eat the mouse if he tries to get away from him.

Let me quote a few verses or so from the Holy Qur'an, chapter 7, verse 27, which refers to the so-called American Negro and any Black, Brown or Yellow man on this earth: "O children of Adam..." reads the 27th verse in the 7th chapter, "...let not the devil seduce you, as he expelled your parents from the garden, pulling off from them their clothes that he might show them their shame. He surely sees you, he as well as his host, from whence you see them not. Surely we have made the devils the friends of those who believe not."

In this verse is a warning to you. Today, the devil is pulling off your clothes, having them cut above your knees; having you going around half nude in the public, even in shorts and garments that are even shorter than shorts. He has you going nude.

A Plain Understanding of The Red Dragon

He has you so, you can hardly hide your own shame. When you sit down, it is all you can do to try keeping the people from looking away from your own shame, which was made to be hidden and put in a secret place by nature, but the devil wants you to be tempted, so you will follow them to hell. He puts you in a position to tempt the world and commit evil and indecency so you will share hellfire with them. This is all it's done for.

I warn you, be aware of this evil and indecent people, whose radio and TV is teaching you who they are. You don't have to take my word for it, look at the indecent acts put on the TV for you and your children to stare at. Listen to the indecent love songs they are singing on the radio and TV day and night, 24 hours a day, just for the sake of time to deceive you and tempt you to do evil and filth.

Their women who do such acts have no shame whatsoever. There is no shyness in them and they will commit these acts with a smile and sing the most filthy songs that you ever heard. They will perform the most evil and the most filthy acts which any human being could ever design to be put before people, even if it's too filthy to be acted in secret.   It is now acted before the so-called Negroes' face.

You help pull off your clothes; you're pulling them off as he has advised you to do. You are following his advice; this is his nature. It is not to be charged to him for making you to do these things; it is you who are responsible for your own evil and filthy doings.

I say, women of my nation, regardless to what white women wear, I say to you, pull down your dress and wear a modest dress if you ever want to join on to your people and be recognized as decent and intelligent people on this planet earth; pull down your dress.

THE WAR OF ARMAGEDDON

My dear people, who have been in the Western Hemisphere in America for 400 long years, the day has arrived wherein you must turn to your own, your own God and your people so you may be able to see the hereafter. The hereafter means after the Holy war or after Armageddon or after the war between Satan and Almighty God. This is what it means when we say the hereafter; it means after the war between right and wrong has been fought.

This war is oftentimes called a war between God and the Devil. The Devil seeks to hold supremacy over God since he has ruled the people for 6,000 years. He desires to continue trying to hold his place as a ruler of the people and seek to bring before the people every opposition that he possibly can to destroy their hearts and their minds toward the worship and obedience to Almighty God Allah.

Here in the Western Hemisphere in America, where there is 22 million original Black people living, whose fathers suffered slavery for around 300 long years, has caused us to believe in the enemy or adversary of God, the real devil himself; consequently, it is hard today to get our people to disbelieve in the devil and believe in Almighty

God, because they never knew anything of God or the devil. They only had the teachings by the slave-master of the slave master, and he was careful to conceal himself so they might not know who he is; therefore, it was impossible for them to learn who God was and who was the devil.

These are really two god's. The devil is a God himself, as mentioned by Jesus in the New Testament, that he is the God of this world, the prince of the power of air. This is true that the Devil has been the ruler for 6,000 years and the God of this world. This world means the world of the Devil, under his rule. The people forgot the Real True God and the way to that True God, because the Devil will not teach the people. Again, in the parable of the fig tree which Jesus, as the book says, cursed. It was also a sign of this world; whereas, this world has never produced converts to the Will of Almighty God, Allah. Never has any so-called American Negro been taught by white people to believe in Almighty God Allah and His true religion, Islam. Only in higher organizations, or we say, Masonry, there is a little teachings which they are taught most of this particular order with the teachings of Almighty God, Allah, but you have to pay a lot of money to become a 33rd degree Mason; consequently, you are absolutely a victim, as Isaiah teaches you. You buy that which does not bring you any good. That kind of teaching does not gain you the hereafter. We must have something that is pure. A Mason cannot be a good Mason unless he knows the Holy Qur'an and follows it's teachings. This book is the only book that will make a true Mason. The Bible won't make you a true one. I say, if you are a true Muslim for real, then alright, let's have it in the open and not in secret.

Of these things I warn you who are listening, that the time is now ripe and is at hand, that everything, everything of good or bad must be made known. We are living in the end of this world, the judgement of this world. These are the days of judgement mentioned in the Bible, as the days of judgement or the days of the resurrection of the dead. These days represent years and not just a little 24 hour day as you know them to be, they mean years. The years of the judgement or resurrection of the dead, we are in those days now.

The coming of Allah and the teaching of Islam to we, who have been lost from our kind, native land and our country, for the past 400 years, means the judgement. God doesn't come until the judgement or until the end of the world of Satan, as you have it written in the Bible, prophesied throughout the Bible and also mentioned absolutely in

Thessalonians, that God comes after the working of Satan, the Devil. After he has did all that he possibly can do of evil, then God comes after allowing him to go to the full or giving him the freedom to try and take all the people with him to hell if possible.

These are the days now in which we are living. I want you to understand my dear people. You are actually not in the way of the truth; you have not actually believed it. The time has now come that even if you would just turn to Almighty God, you would enjoy salvation or heaven in this world, and in the hereafter you are sure of the heaven.

Even in this life, God gives the righteous a peace of mind and contentment. He is the Protector of the righteous after He makes His appearance, in religion. The judgement will come and their will be a great separation at the judgement. This is true, but you don't believe that you are now living in such a time: that there is a great separation now in the workings.

When you first heard that their was someone in your midst given the names, which to you sounded similar to foreign or Indian names, such as Karriem, Biar, Muhammad, Farrakhan, Hassan, Hazim, Ali and many names that you are now hearing. These names are being given to your own people and they are being called by these names. You are so dead to the knowledge of self, kind, the knowledge of the truth and the true God, that you don't even pay no attention to it.

You even make fun of these names although you never heard of these names before; therefore, are called foolish or fools in the Bible and the Holy Qur'an, because of not grabbing a dictionary to see what such names mean. When you learn that these names mean good names of God, as mentioned in most all teaching of religion, that God has 99 names and the one hundredth is Allah, which means that He's all of the names of good. The Bible teaches you, if you will agree with me, that no one will escape or will see the hereafter, unless he has the name of Almighty God, Allah. You have to have one of these 99 names.

God has come, as your Bible teaches you, and has given to us His own Holy names; they are Holy names. I want you to remember that; they are Holy names. Not one definition, or your interpretation, as you may call it, of these names can you look up, which does not mean a good name or a divine name. These things are true; look in your dictionary and you will find them, the meaning of them.

Many of you foolish or fools will even laugh at hearing one of you being called Muhammad. Muhammad means Praised and Praise Worthy. It's a name of God Almighty, which means that God is Praised and God is worthy to be praised. When this name is given to you, just remember that you are a person who is called praised and you are worthy of praise. All divine people, I mean the black people, as Almighty God has taught me, in the person of Master Fard Muhammad, are entitled to these names, because, as the Bible teaches you in the Psalms, that we all are God's and the children of the heavenly Kingdom.

You are the children in knowledge, that's what it means, the lost found children in the knowledge of God. It does not mean the age of you, but in the knowledge of you in God; you are nothing but children and that is true. They are given these names, because by nature they are from God and they are of God and they deserve to be called Gods too. They are God's. They came from God and they're the children of God. You find it mentioned in the New Testament: To them whom He reveals Himself, referring to the Jesus, that they became the son's of God.

You are very ignorant to be laughing and making fun of such names as divine, the Supreme Being's names, because of the white man, who enslaved your fathers and made them blind, deaf and dumb, to themselves. You follow what they have revealed to you and not what God has revealed. You have taken them for Gods and you worship them as God, as it is written again in the Revelations, and elsewhere in the Bible, that you worship Devils.

This is the kind of a thing that Allah has come to make manifest, so that you may turn to your own God, be saved and see the hereafter. Allah is well able to take care of you. Fear not that you will be the looser if you believe in Allah. Allah has always, in the past and at the present, taken care of His own people. He's never too weak to take care of them. You have read in the scripture and the histories of the past where God protected His own people from the evil doers and the destruction of the evil doers. How well He is able to do that today.

He created the heavens and the earth and everything in it is His. He has power over everything; this you must understand. You laugh at the name Allah, because the white man never taught you that the Divine Supreme Being's proper name is Allah. He doesn't want you to believe in Islam. This is true.

They don't want you to believe in Islam though their are some white people in America who actually believe in Islam. I would say there are many of them. They run into the thousands and they actually believes in the teachings of Islam, but by nature, they are not real Muslims or they are not the children of God, but they believe in Almighty God, Allah, and His teaching. These are the teachings you find written in the book which says that a remnant of them will be saved. If they hold fast and do not loose their salvation by hating to hear the real truth of them, they will be removed from out of the area where there will be war between God and the Devil.

Only the people who opposes God, He will fight and bring to a naught. It is not the people who do not oppose God and do not teach other people to oppose Him, but it is that vicious and evil people that teaches against the belief in Almighty God and teach other people to hate those that believe in Almighty God, Allah. These are the people who receives severe judgement of God.

I warn you my people, since I see that you don't understand too well, that you should come to the knowledge of the truth. You should listen to me and you should follow me, but you are a little too proud to do so at the present time; however, a thing is coming, which God will cause to take place and you will be forced to believe and submit. On that day, you will be shamed to do so, because you had already rejected the truth and refused to follow the inviter of the truth; consequently, you will be shamed and disgraced to come to the inviter of the truth.

To you my friends who are [reading] this, this is the judgement. America is headed for total divine judgement. This is the fourth beast mentioned in Daniel that God will destroy first, and the other beast, their lives will be prolonged for a time and time in our time. This is also known to all of the scientists and scholars on the scripture. It's well known that this is the symbolic beast which Daniel saw. The same beast is mentioned in the Revelation of the Bible, rising up and becoming stronger than all his predecessor, but was destroyed, because he rose up against Almighty God, Allah, to pitch a war against Him.

He went forth to gather people, as the Revelation says, to that mighty battle between Almighty God and Satan. He gathered people to help him fight and oppose God setting up a kingdom of peace and of righteousness. This is the one, America, and she is now under divine chastisement and will end up into fire. That is known. There is no protection; no defense from divine judgement. You can't fight God and win. You have nothing to fight and oppose Him.

God fights you with the forces of nature and the forces of nature, you have no control over. If he would send a blast of heat from the sun, He could lick you up without any further ado over you. He could cause the earth to shake and bring down every one of your villages, towns and cities throughout the land, in the twinkling of and eye. He could bring down hail and snow from the north and destroy you with cold bitter, bitter cold weather, as He did people in the past. The Holy Qur'an mentioned people to you that were destroyed by cold weather, a cold blasting of wind for 8 days, 8 days and 7 nights. These winds came out of the North with freezing temperatures, destroyed the people. You cannot fight God; it's impossible.

My friends, I want to say to you, do not hate the Messenger for teachings you the truth. You should be glad to hear a Messenger of God teaching you the truth in these days and times. It makes you aware of what you are doing.

Ninevah heard the message of Almighty God Allah coming to them from Ghana; they repented and they had forsaken their luxury, sat in the dust to repent of their evil and God gave Ninevah an extension of life. No, I don't think you will do these things, because it's already written that you would do what you're doing. I don't think you will repent, though if you would repent, God would accept your repentance, and maybe get you through your children in the future, who will not repent.. You're probably already the children of the future, who have not or who have refused to repent.

Today, I warn you my [readers], you are living in the day of the judgement and America is on the list of God to be destroyed, as God has Already taught and warned me and taught me the way He will destroy America.

In 1958, Washington, I said that by 1970, the resurrection of the poor, lost and found, original people of the earth, the Blackman, would all be resurrected by that time here in America. You see more signs of that truth coming true now than you ever have seen before.

You see the people, the darker people here, giving in to the truth of Almighty God that I'm teaching. You see them paying more attention to it today than they ever have; regardless to the storm of opposition that has been created against me and my followers, which I cares not, because I'm sure that I must suffer the same thing as other prophets. I don't call myself a prophets, I am a Messenger of God. You don't need a prophet today. All you need is the Messenger; for this is the end of the prophets, because what they predicted is now making itself manifest; so, it is the end of them.

I'm teaching you and I do say that I'm the Messenger and that these things are now manifesting themselves, that the so-called American Negro will bow to the Will of Almighty God, Allah. They are divine people of God and have been mislead and have went astray from the Divine Supreme Being.

From the white slave-master's guidance and his teaching, it has caused this poor people to forget God, caused this people to not even know themselves, has caused this people today to be fighting and opposing their own salvation, when they should be running into it by the hundreds of thousands.

The enemy knows these things, that you now stand at the door of your salvation. It has come to you in the teachings that I am giving to you today; this is it. You must have the name of Almighty God; a name that will live. The only name that will live, is a name of God. You must have that. You must know today that you must join on to your own people. You must know today that you must have some of this earth that you can call your own. You must know today that you cannot make friends with this people and with God at the same time. You must know that there is no friendship in them for you and me. You must know that they are the adversaries of God. You must know that they are determined to carry you with them to their doom, despite Almighty God's calling and offer to you for heaven at once.

I say to you, my beloved people, [who are reading this today], fly for your lives and stop trying to become one of them or forcing them to accept you as one of them. Fly from them into the arms of Almighty God, Allah, as it is written, His hands and arms are stretched out still to you. Stop being tempted by Satan's advertisement of filth. Pull your dress down woman and stop going around walking the streets with your dress above your knees, showing the nation your shame. It is nothing but filth that has been offered to you by Satan and you are swallowing it by the wholesale.

Any husband that will walk along with his wife, seeing her dress above her knees, is a poor husband. He doesn't value his own property, his wife.   He doesn't value the property which is in that wife. I say, you husbands who allow such things as this should be punished yourself.

THE BEAST OF REVELATIONS

Negro is a slang name given by the slave-masters and they continue calling my people by that name today. They will continue doing so until my people learn that they are not Negroes, but are actually the lost-found member of a great nation, the original nation of the earth, the first people on the earth. They are from, according to the word of Allah to me, a tribe by the name Shabazz.

The American so-called Negro has been here in the Western Hemisphere for a little over 400 years. This is the length of time that they are suppose to have stayed in the Western Hemisphere. According to the prophesy made to Abraham by Almighty God, Whose proper name is Allah: That Know of a surety, that thy people shall be a stranger in a land that is not theirs and shall serve strangers for 400 years and at the end of that time I will judge that nation and bring again thy people into this land where you and I now stand, I will return them....

The returning of a lost and found member of a nation to his rightful place among his own people has absolutely been mentioned many times throughout the Bible. The Old Testament refers to such a lost people and the seeking and finding of that member. It almost begins in Genesis and ends in Revelations under the symbolic account of the Beast. The Messenger is under a symbolic name, according to the characteristics of the truth, as a Lamb trying to give birth in the midst of beasts. This is a very beautiful picture given in the Revelations and also in Genesis.

The picture of the enemy is made and symbolized with the name of the Beast, but under the name of a serpent.   This particular name, serpent, goes throughout the Bible and refers to the enemy of the righteous.   The poor Messenger is fighting a vicious beast in the Revelations who seeks to destroy the child as soon as it is born, which means this: The beast seeks to take away the truth, destroy the truth from coming to the child or prevent the child from believing it as soon as it is told to him or taught. This is the better and the most intelligent answer to that particular symbolic Beast opposing the Woman and her child in the Revelation.

The Woman represents a Messenger who was pregnant with the truth, trying to convert the people who know not God unto God with the truth with which she's pregnant. As the beast is the enemy, not a four-footed beast, but these beasts are men.

They are a Nation who is opposed to the truth, with which the Messenger is pregnant, and seeks to take his converts away from him as fast as they are converted to God Almighty with that truth, which God has put into him.

That truth has now caused the Messenger to be pregnant with truth like a woman pregnant with a child, and an evil beast, savage beast is set in the bushes across somewhere, under a rock, cliff or in the bushes, waiting to pounce upon the little child, destroy it and eat it as soon as it is born. This is an ugly picture given to the enemies of God and His religion of truth. It is true though that they have similar characteristics.

A wicked and evil person, hater of God and His truths is like a wild savage beast. The woman [is like a] lamb or a sheep, which means that the Messenger was like a lamb who does not have absolute protection in the midst of the wild beast preventing it from being destroyed or eaten. His only protection is by the shepherd's watchful eye and the steel which the shepherd has for keeping the beast away from destroying his sheep.

Jesus also made mention these wicked opposers of the truth in the [Bible], 23rd chapter of Matthew, under the symbolic name of serpents in the 33rd verse of the 23rd chapter. It reads like this, "Ye serpents, ye generation of vipers, how can he escape the damnation of hell?" Remember the serpents here are the disbelievers of the truth and haters of the truth, haters of the prophet, who is the truth bearer.

We are in the midst of such people today. We are in the midst of a people who are opposed. These serpents that Jesus referred to here were leaders of the people, those who are suppose to have been the guides. Again, these serpents refer to religious leaders. In the same chapter, he says here that, "...behold, I send unto you prophets, wise men, scribes: and some of them ye shall kill and crucify; some of them shall ye scourge in your synagogues, persecute them from city to city: That upon you may come all the righteous blood shed upon the earth, from the blood of righteous A'bel unto to the blood of Zacharias son of Barachias, whom ye slew between the temple and the altar. Verily I say unto you, All these things shall come upon this generation."

All of those things, the destruction, damnation and the hell, did not come to the people who opposed Jesus 2,000 years ago, this prophesy refers to the end of that evil generation or that evil race of people who has opposed God and His prophets for thousands of years. It goes back to the Garden of Eden where they opposed God there: the serpent, and turned his own people into hypocrites and caused them to be cast out with the serpent. This goes on up until God strikes the serpent in the Revelation with a war, and brings him to an end in a lake of fire, he and his false prophets. This is the same serpent who deceived the people of Paradise and the same serpent who will deceive the people in the last days and cause the people to prepare themselves to fight and oppose Almighty God and His angels, His prophets and His saints, in the last days, over the dead, the mentally dead, whom they have killed of the knowledge of themselves and of the knowledge of the Almighty God of truth and justice.

Islam is being preached in the midst of you throughout the country today. This is the religion that's prophesied in the Bible by the prophets, even up into your last book, the Revelations, and throughout the Holy Qur'an, that it would come at the end of the white man's time.

This day and time in which you and I live is the time of a change of rulership and of earth. It is a time of great separation. It is a time of great trouble. It is a time Jesus prophesied of that would come upon the Nation. In the 24th chapter, this time and trouble that you and I have seen and are now entering into, must come to pass. The Nations going to war with each other. All disagreeing with each other, as Daniel refer to them as the conflicts of change. All of this must come to pass to bring about the truth and a kingdom of peace, freedom, justice and equality for the Nation of the earth and especially the righteous, but there are a few people, only a few, that know and understand the time that they are living in.

Islam is the religion of God. It is the religion that all must believe in before ever they can see the Hereafter. I don't mean after you are dead in the grave; the Hereafter that I'm referring to is only the hereafter the war of Armageddon, the Holy war that will be fought between the great religions of the earth. It is that war to bring about the knowledge of the true religion, the power of God, the power of the holy people and the power of that religion of truth mentioned or rather is prophesied to come in the sixty first Surah/chapter of the Holy Qur'an in these words, "He it is Who sent His Messenger with the guidance and the true religion, that He may make it overcome the religions, all of them, though the polytheists may be adverse." Islam is not in the last day to tolerate false religion. It is to overcome all false religion, regardless to the opposition it may meet, because it is the truth.

There is 90 percent of the foolish ignorant preachers of the so-called Negroes, who never studies Islam and have no knowledge of even what the word Islam means. The word Islam mean one who has submitted or we say, the word Islam means entire submission to the will of God and if any man believe in the God of truth and righteousness and desire to be His servant, he must submit to the will of God to be a Muslim and this is the only and the final religion of the earth: a religion of entire submission to the Will of God or the doing of the Will of God.

This is the religion prophesied by all the prophets that would come in the last days. Here today, I am being opposed by my own people, the so-called religious leaders who have not learned the secret meaning or the science of their religion, which they profess to believe in - Christianity. They don't know what's actually being preached in Christianity.

For instance, you say you are Christian, Christian means something that is crystallized; let us Christian something into one or crystallized into one. You also say that it means being Christ-like. If it means Christ-like, if it means to be one in Christ, I say, remember that the Muslims then are the only true Christians of the earth. They are the

One people. They are absolutely one and one into Allah, the Great Mahdi prophesied to come in the Bible and Holy Qur'an. In the Bible, they call Him the Messiah, in the Holy Qur'an, the 22nd chapter, they prophesy Him coming under the name of Mahdi. The Mahdi means one who is Self-Independent, Self-Guided, coming to guide others. This Great One that they have been predicting to come for the last 2,000 years, is now on the scene.

I have met with Him and He has given to me the knowledge of truth. I am not boasting about it, I only want you to see, you my people, the truth and not continue being blind, deaf and dumb, like you have been made. You have never been taught the real truth. This you will admit to me in secret, you know that, but in the open you are just the opposite.

Today we have before us, the real truth. We have the true religion regardless to your opposition to it and you won't be able to drive it out as you desire. As Reverend Bauler there in Atlanta, Georgia, [one] Sunday morning, 8:30 on the air, who indirectly asked for help to drive the Muslims out of the city of Atlanta.

Reverend Bauler, my poor blind, deaf and dumb brother of Georgia, I was born in the state of Georgia Reverend Bauler. I was brought up there and was a strong man when I left there. I know you, I know my people in Georgia, I know my people's slave master in Georgia. I'm well acquainted with everything in Georgia, that goes for the two people white and black. I'm well acquainted with the history of the religion that you are now so sincerely trying to defend for the sake and praise of the white man. I say you are fighting fire and don't know it, but it might stain your eyes after a while, and it might leave a scar upon you that is incurable.

I'm so sorry that the lost and found people of the nation of Islam, from the Tribe of Shabazz, have no knowledge of the true religion of God, or have no knowledge of the time in which we are living; for they are living in the time of a great separation and living in a time of great enlightenment. The truth has come to you. Know that the God is now in the midst and is directing His truth regardless to opposition. We suffer persecution; we suffer beatings; nevertheless, we have the truth and we will be the winners in the end.

I'm so sorry that you, Reverend Bauler, don't understand that you are leading your people directly to hell and destruction and don't know it your own self. There will be no such thing as the religion that you preach today - Christianity -

existing in the Hereafter. It is not even accepted by God. He don't want that kind of religion which was organized by the European race of people, after the death of Jesus.

Jesus did not preach this type of religion, he preached Islam, which means entire submission to the Will of God, his Father, he says in your Bible. Submit to God and enter into His peace; this is the religion Islam.

The nation of Islam today as you see, Reverend Bauler, are not building battle ships and airplanes covering the sky with a lot of planes, deadly submarines, boats crawling on the bottom of the ocean, they are not doing anything like that. We are a people of peace and the God of peace is on our side. We don't need any such weapons to fight the enemy with. There is more artillery out there in the forces of nature to fight an enemy than we can absolutely find enough use for.

God Almighty, Whose proper name is Allah, have power over the forces of nature. He has power over man. We have been told not to carry weapons and we don't carry them. We don't depend on no kind of weapons for our defense.

Reverend Bauler, we are in Atlanta; we will not be rooted up and driven out, we are the righteous and the earth belongs to the righteous. Mr. Bauler, I do think you should feel shame and disgrace before your black, blind, deaf and dumb people of Georgia to even stand before them calling yourself a preacher of righteous, a preacher of justice, a preacher of equality, and freedom of your people, in the name of God and then [speak about that which you know not] before you ever meet another man who say's that he is from God, preaching freedom, justice and equality for his black brothers and sisters of America, and understand what he's absolutely preaching. But no, too proud you are to meet that man, too guilty of not having the nerve, knowledge and the wisdom to meet him and fight him with truth. You don't have that truth to fight him with.

You have heard this truth; yet, you don't want to meet me. You only want to show to your friends, the white man of Georgia and of the country, that "I am with you..." and are willing to destroy Elijah and his followers if you help me. That is the same thing that they said of Jesus, the religious leaders uniting and went to Pilate and told Pilate, "away with Jesus, kill Jesus, crucify him and give us - if you want to just free one - of these two men. Free the murderer and kill Jesus."

This is the cry of the preachers today: Get rid of Elijah and his followers; help us and we will cast them out. You will do that, or you will try doing it. You won't be successful, but you will try doing it, because you're just that foolish enough to do anything to destroy any people of yours that the white man say he don't like.

We are some in the midst of you that maybe you might not like, but I say, if you don't like us, leave alone, because you most certainly are going to find yourself playing with fire, and a very hot fire at that.

We are the righteous, we are in your midst showing you how to live the life of the righteous, preaching the truth, the salvation of my own black people who have been made blind, deaf and dumb and deprived of freedom, justice and equality and you profess to be their leader of righteous and a preacher of God and His Christ and are actually condemning freedom, justice, and equality for your people, to the inducement of hell.

THE DRAGON

This Almighty God, Allah, has taught me in the person of Master Fard Muhammad, to Whom praise is due forever, for coming in this part of the world, giving to us the knowledge of self, the knowledge of others, the knowledge of God, the knowledge of the devil and making clear and understandable that which we had been saying before, but the truth of which we were unable to understand.

Today we are thankful; those of us who have heard this truth coming from the mouth of Almighty God, Allah, in the person of Master Fard Muhammad. It is that which we had never heard, that which we did not even hope to hear. We are thankful and give praise to Almighty God Allah forever, for His coming. We are happy, regardless to our affliction which we are now suffering, we are still happy, because we have every hope and assurance that one day we will also be happy and there will be no afflictions.

We don't look forward, as the Christian preachers preach, to die and go into the earth and rise again out of the earth and get joy out of a life as a spirit. We expects all of this joy in this life and not a spirit life; for Almighty God, Allah, has revealed to us the truth.

We have been teaching on true religion, which is a great subject, and shall continue after it. We are going to pick up what we have been writing on for the last few weeks: the great dragon of the 12th chapter, of Revelations in the Bible.

The name given there is to the devil, according to the Bible in the 9th verse of the 12th chapter. It says "...the great dragon was cast out, that old serpent, called the Devil, and Satan, which decieveth the whole world: he was cast out into the earth, and his angels were cast out with him." This I can say truthfully for the last few weeks. That on writing on this particular subject and 12th chapter of Revelation, you that have been reading it may now understand who the dragon really is.

The dragon is that particular person or people who are called the Devil or the Satan. This particular chapter, the 12th chapter, gives us a good knowledge that this [Dragon] is not a spook or spirit or something other than human. The Dragon is a human being and we find it here in the 3rd verse of the same chapter reading like this: "And there appeared another wonder in heaven; and behold a great red dragon, having 7 heads and 10 horns, and 7 crowns upon his head." Seven crowns upon his head: This can't refer to a savage, 4 footed beast with legs. It cannot refer to some spirit. This refers to a human or being, and the name, dragon, given is according to the characteristics or work of that being.

This is a very good interpretation or proper term for the name, dragon, because the particular wicked characteristics for which the prophet gave this name was to drags people, the good people away from good and induce evil instead of good for them. He's ever dragging the righteous from the path of righteousness, away from Allah, the true and living God, and deceiving them as it teaches us here in the 9th verse, he deceived the whole world.

No snake or beast can deceive us; it takes another human being with an intelligent brain like ours or one with more intelligence than ours to deceive us. When one deceives another in the human family, he's given credit that he has a little more brains or a little more skill in tricking the other one, making the other one a prisoner or prey to his knowledge. So it is with the serpent or the dragon here referred to in Genesis and also the Revelation.

The first and the last book mentioned this serpent. The serpent here is a human being. He has the voice of a man or people in the garden of paradise. He could even speak Adam's own language and he understood the language of God; therefore, it really was not a snake as someone has made you believe in the past to blind you further to the knowledge of actually who the serpent really is.

They even said the snake use to walk; moreover, having the language to speak and converse with human beings, also has to be reckoned with. If he walked on 4 feet or on a hundred feet, how about the use of that language? Could he speak our language or deceive us and he being a reptile? Alligators go on 4 feet, and there's other reptiles today that are crawling, walking on 4 feet, and swimming and walking, but they don't deceive us; they're not smart enough. Nature didn't give them that kind of intelligent brain to equal our intelligent brains.

This particular character under the name, serpent or dragon, mentioned here in the Bible, in Genesis and in Revelation, refers to a human being or many beings. The reason the pronoun "he" is given to him here, or he's referred to singularly, is due to the fact that the Revelation refers to the very head of the dragon people or the serpent like people's characteristics. This particular dragon is the head of the nation or race; therefore, it is mentioned clearly enough for you and I to understand here in the 7th verse that he had 7 heads and 10 horns, with 7 crowns upon his head.

The heads of that particular serpent or dragon is being taught to us in symbolic language to represent something material. These heads represent governments, peoples or actually places where power of the serpent like people or dragon like people rules.

Many have interpreted the 7 heads here as being the 7 hills upon which Rome is built and that actually the dragon being the pope of Rome has been interpreted. I'm not going to deviate from that meaning, because it is clear that it refers to some heads or some head under such title or characteristics of that particular power, which is ruling and is opposed to the power of righteousness and justice; therefore, the head of the dragon is the head of the Church of Christianity and also the Jew's ruling power of the Caucasian race, according to the way that it is given and interpreted by scientists of religion of Christianity and others. So, here we are dealing with a people who's characteristics are that of a serpent or a snake: very evil and tricky. They are a tricky people who love to deceive the people, as the 9th verse of the twelfth chapter warns, that he deceive the whole world.

Snakes are not capable of deceiving the whole world. It takes human beings to fool or deceive other human beings, as I just said; therefore, this refers to a people who have deceived the whole world. We don't know of any other people who has the wisdom or the brains to deceive the other people of the earth, but the Caucasian race, who have actually been the rulers of the people of earth for the past 6,000 years.

It is this race who rules; it is this race who has ruled, just opposite to right. They have been a people who has ruled the original people of the earth under a rule of evil, wickedness, bloodshed and under deceit. This particular people are now today referred to as serpents and dragon; the great red dragon that was found also in heaven.

Heaven here could mean the whole earth or in the most Holy part of the earth. If that is referring to the Holy part of the earth, it means Arabia. Arabia is and has been the most Holiest part of the entire earth, because she can boast of the very origin and birth of most of the prophets of which we have history. Therefore, the holy or religious people have been found in that part of the world or earth every since the creation of Adam 6,000 years ago.

This red dragon, if it means the Caucasian race or the head of Christianity in Rome, we find in Arabia today and all over the planet earth. Since the 9th verse says that they deceived the whole world, it stands true if they have now gotten power and a hold on that particular country, enabling them to work there and carry out their own way of civilization in certain parts of that holy and sacred land and people, then it proves beyond a shadow of a doubt that the 12th chapter and the symbolic serpent and dragon there only means the Caucasian race and the religion which is capable of deceiving the people.

It is true that they have spread their religion all over the earth, as well as Islam having also gotten it's powerful hold on the people of the earth, but Islam does not boast that she has ruled and attracted the people of earth a hundred percent for the last 2,000 or rather for nearly the last 14,000 years.

Christianity has gotten a hold of the people throughout the entire earth and there are many Muslims who have also went from Islam and accepted Christianity. We see this serpent or red dragon as being the power and head of the Caucasian race, working deceitfully and deceiving the people of the original nation, the darker people throughout the earth.

There is now a great change or reform coming, and a new religion or new conception of Islam to suit the need and time it is now in. A complete new Islam is coming to the people. The God of Islam is removing the opposition to Islam today by going directly to the head of the opposing religions and people. That is what we are now and have entered into; it is a war between right and wrong. We know that Allah is true and the only True God. We know that Islam is the only true religion, which means entire submission to the Will of Almighty God Allah. We know that, and the world of infidels know that. It has started now in America among the so-called Negroes.

The lost and found members of that great Asiatic Black Nation, who has been here lost from their own people for 400 years, absolutely being deprived of intermixing with their own kind and deprived of their own kind coming among them to teach them of themselves and their religion, Islam. This is absolutely true, and the world over knows that. Let us look again at the work of this particular red dragon.

The 4th verse says, "...his tail drew the third part of the stars of heaven, and did cast them to the earth...." Now this 3rd part of stars here represent not only the 3rd part of the people of the righteous, but it could refers to the scholars or scientists of Islam; whereas, a 3rd of them had agreed or will agree on the side of the dragon. Not that it actually will be done, for this is only a suggestion. When we say stars, we're referring to human beings. It means that particular character of one who has achieved a great height of education or into whatever the case may be. They have become more smarter or wiser in it than anyone else; consequently, we call them stars. They are absolutely more qualified than the general public or the common people of that race or nation. That's why I said it must refer to the scientist. If it refers to the people, it also stands true that the dragon probably will carry a third of the civilized people of earth with him, other than his own, because he has deceived the whole entire world so.

As he has deceived the whole world, it is possible that he can carry along with him a third of that particular world even after he has been made manifest to the world, that he is a deceiver. Since they have to prove [or be convinced] that he is a deceiver, he could keep and hold them in subjection to his deceit or power, deceiving a third of those whom he had already deceived.

The Revelation further says that this particular dragon or the devil here, stood before a woman which was ready to be delivered, to devour her child as soon as it was born. This woman that the dragon stands before can easily be understood. If the dragon is people then the woman is got to be people. If he stands before her, it means that he is hindering her, as one in front of another, to impede the other's progress in the race or in going forward. This is what it's referred to here: The dragon stands before the woman to impede her progress or to destroy her progress in delivering her child as she had planned.

The woman could stand for a messenger of God who is pregnant with the conversion or the resurrection of a people or great nation of people, or it could refer to the coming of God in person, which the dragon is hindering. He stands before God to keep him from performing his purpose or duty of deliver a people who are now ready to be delivered. Again, let us look at this possibility of the dragon hindering the birth of that child and his evil intentions to devour it as soon as it is born.

He watches it; he's before her and he intends to be at the birth of the child, because he doesn't intend for the child to be born and then grow up; so, he's waiting for the birth of this child in order to destroy it as soon as it is born; that will keep it from growing up and coming to maturity. If it ever comes to maturity, then he would not be able to destroy the child. He wants to get it in it's infancy.

This refers to here [America] if we understand it clearly, of which I believe we do. For according to the time, the work, the history of the prophets in the past, their followers and according to our understanding of the Last Messenger and his followers before the general judgement of the wicked, it refers to none other than the American so-called Negroes. They are ready to be resurrected. Their time has arrived that they should be resurrected, according to this same book the Revelation.

In another place, it says that it's the time of the dead, that they should rise and be given knowledge, in words [so to speak]. This chapter mentions this particular time as being the time of the dead, meaning that they, a people that is mentally dead, should rise and come to life. However, here stands a dragon or an enemy to that people to prevent their rise or resurrection into the knowledge of God and the knowledge of the devil. They stand ready to destroy them. This means none other than the people we are now living with here in America. We find that we are hindered here in becoming converts to Almighty God, Allah, and the religion of Islam.

What's going on in Los Angeles today it isn't a trial of my followers before the courts of the infidels and before the people that have proven themselves enemies of my fathers and myself and all of my people - the darker people of earth. They have proven themselves openly that they are the enemies of black man.

What Will Be The End of America?

According to history, the breaking up or change of the OLD for the NEW, has always brought about the persecution of the representatives of the new. Again, according to history, the old was the loser.

Allah has taught me of the great persecution in the days of the grafting of the Caucasian race (white race), out of the original Black Nation. And the only solution was total separation. Gen. 3:23; Deut. 32:8; Matt. 25:32. Holy Qur'an 2:36, 38; 7:34. The proud Negro leadership is blind and cannot see that these are the days of separation. Therefore, they help persecute the Muslims (the righteous) and think they are beloved of God for doing so. They are self-made, self-sent, authorized by the devils on a script of paper. For such hypocrites, read: Matt. 23:13, 29, 34. ...And when the dragon saw that he was cast into the earth, he persecuted the woman (the Messenger of God) which brought forth the man ...Rev. 12:13.

Persecution is the bitter pill for the new converts of a new change from the old. The old never wants to give way to the new. We are now in a change of worlds or civilizations. The previous change of governments, and the persecution of the Apostles and their followers, at the hand of the old civilization, are put into the scriptures for our learning and warning of that final change of worlds.

Pharaoh and his dealings with Israel was a sign of what you and I are facing today. Mentioned under the Bible's last book, called the Revelation of John, is a very appropriate name, according to the character's nature and work, the "beast." They (white race) also once lived a life of part beast and part human. The symbolical "beast" of Revelation.

The so-called Negroes who refuse to believe in the false religion of the "beast" (Christianity), his name, his mark, or to worship him, suffer persecution. This persecution serves as a trial to both the believing Muslims, so-called Negroes and the disbelieving so-called Negroes. The persecution of the Muslims in America is being carried on more for the purpose of frightening the others from accepting Allah, Islam, and the true religion of God, than to change those who already believe in Allah and Islam.

As we see and Hear, the poor, devil-made black preachers are more an enemy to the Muslims than the devils themselves. The devils are wise as we are, to what will be the end of their persecution of the Muslims. They know the black preachers and black educated so-called Negroes are blind, deaf and dumb to the time and the end of these things. The black preachers and so-called educated Negroes are looking towards the white man as defenders for them against Allah and the Muslims. This class among the so-called Negroes are now being made manifest to those of the poor un-learned Negroes as their worse enemies.

For thirty years, we the Muslims, have been persecuted by the so-called Negro preachers and so-called Negro politicians. They care not for the love of Allah (God) and the Truth (Islam). Their love and worship is for the devils, though they are told in Revelation 9:20, that they should not worship devils. The doom of one party and the disgrace of the other will not be delayed; it is very near.

America's rotten government of injustice to the so-called Negro Muslims have not caused us to weaken in faith, but has strengthened us, and has given us more converts. For Allah desires to show Himself as God to these devils and our disbelieving people; that there is no God but He and I am His Messenger. The American white man ignores his own law of justice when it comes to the so-called Negroes. They are especially unjust to the Muslims whom they are afraid will win the so-called Negroes to Allah, that He (Allah) may bless and deliver them from their merciless hands.

In Monroe, Louisiana, the devils were again made manifest, that there is no law or justice under the flag of America for the black men and women that they will respect. After the defense lawyer, Sharpe, had proved by the laws of the U.S. Court, the innocence of the Muslims, the court and its blood-thirsty, human-like beast, ignored it and sent the Muslims to prison. The defending lawyer (Sharpe) was so surprised at such open action of the court, ignoring its own law of justice, that he stood on the floor of the court before the inhuman devil Jury and wept. For he never thought his white devil teachers and instructors of their law could ignore it, without even the thought that they were disgracing themselves and casting aside their own laws. We put up $19,000 in Monroe, Louisiana, as bond money for the Muslims, besides several thousand dollars to the lawyers and traveling expenses.

We did this also for my son, Wallace Muhammad. For four years, the Muslims paid out more than $16,000 to obtain justice and freedom for my son, who was never a citizen of America and cannot ever be one according to what really constitutes an American citizen. Will the U.S.A. have my son, Akbar Muhammad, arrested and returned to the U.S.A., claiming that he is a citizen of America and must take part in her defense in case of war; whom I have enrolled in the University of Al-Ahzar, ., Egypt?

It is very clear that the Government of America does not mean to free us, indeed, without causing a lot trouble. I am asking for our freedom to return to our own people or give us, the entire 20 million, a few states here, where we can go for self with a little help for the next 20 or 25 years. Give us something to fight for other than just a job that you make for us. We will make our own jobs if given the proper chance and place. We don't want to be free slaves for you any longer! Let us go free for ourselves! (11/16/61)

AMERICA WILL DESTROY HERSELF

2-1-62

Separation of the two, (Negro and white) is the only solution to the every growing problem of "What must be done with the Negroes?" Both the so-called Negroes and the whites do not seem to want to let go one another. While the separation of the two races would be an act of wisdom and justice; on the other hand, to force integration, which means socializing, inter-marrying of the two races (black and white) and the eventual swallowing up of the so-called Negroes' race by their white slave-masters, or mongrelizing the two races, this will destroy the respect of the society of both, nationally and internationally. Integration is against the wishes of the intelligent thinking group of both races. They want to preserve their races and the respect of their societies.

The government is trying to enforce this wicked and contrary law on the Divine Law and place of God, which will end in revolution and war, and total destruction of the wealth of America. This integration is not the wise and proper way of solving the so-called Negroes' problem in America, but is an outright deceitful and wicked plan toward

Allah for the future of the so-called Negroes. Both are sure to run into trouble with Allah's chastisement, both Negroes and whites, as it is plainly hinted and written in the Bible and Holy Qur'an. (I will gladly point it out to the disputer).

The wise white scientists know it as well as I, and hope to prevent it, but they are out numbered by their wickedly wise. God created two kinds of everything, so it is with man. He didn't intend for them (Negro and white) to mix, and has set a day of reckoning for those who willfully, and knowingly break His natural law in which He hast created man. It is their purpose to try and make Allah, God, a liar, so as to deceive the blind, deaf, and dumb so-called Negroes, as the devil deceived Adam and Eve in the garden of Paradise while knowing fully well that they would lose their place with Allah and a peaceful home if they accepted his advice. So it will be with the so-called American Negroes, who after being offered heaven at once by Allah, accepts the wicked advice and the offer of a temporary enjoyment with racial intermarrying and having sexual intercourse with a people with whom Allah is angry.

He will punish both parties as he did Israel and the people whom Jehovah forbade Israel to intercourse with. Israel was punished, and finally lost the goal which Jehovah had set before her and the deceiving enemies of Israel were destroyed. I warn you to let Israel's history, from the days of Moses to this day, be a lesson to you. REMEMBER, both Israel and the Christians are on the brink of a pit of fire. The best and only solution of this problem of the so-called Negroes is SEPARATION and giving them a start in a territory to themselves, regardless to the ignorant love of the slave for his master.

Take a look at the foolish plan of Martin Luther King for the poor so-called Negroes and how he and his plan were criticized by Mr. James B. Kilpatrick, recently, on the Television program, "Nation's Future." There we saw the man, Rev. King, a college man, a Christian Minister and Pastor, with a plan to take our poor people and himself and throw them at the mercy of an angry Negro-hating mob, to be beaten and killed for nothing; only to be accepted as whites accept whites, in white private-owned places, and finally allow his people to become white, mongrelizing both races. What does he think the intelligent white and black people think of his silly plan? What kind of foolish so-called Negro parents will let such foolish preachers use their babies as a test of the mob's fire? What will those children's think of such parents when they grow up and see the light of truth? Mr. Kilpatrick asked Rev. King,

"Why do you want to integrate and make your race a coffee color, with complete integration, losing your race identity?" He was telling Martin Luther King, in so many words, that you and your race will not cause the white race to lose their identity, but the Negro will lose his. Such slander and mockery coming to the decent and intelligent so-called Negroes, by the ignorant love of a so-called religious leader of his people, is a disgrace.

Such short-sightedness by Rev. King and the NAACP for the so-called Negro of America, is making the nations of the earth, both black and white, laugh us to scorn, to see us, as a race of lazy beggars and great lovers of our enemies. Why doesn't Mr. King and his NAACP organization join with me on a decent plan; a plan that makes sense and one that will make a future for our people.

Ask for separation and some of this good earth that we can call our own, where we can live in peace together, away from those who do not want us. This is the plan of God and it will bring an end to the ever growing trouble between the two races. If the white man, some of them, wanted to colonize us in Central America back in 1867, why not a free territory today, for we will not accept colonization. It is the time of our FREEDOM, and we will not accept anything less!

The NAACP and Mr. King want the freedom of voting, and in this way, they think they will be able to gain equal power in a white man's government and country. A Negro will never be the president under the Stars and Stripes of America. If he did, what could he do but to bow to the wishes of the owners of the Stars and Stripes? Let us seek some stars for our own nation and stop begging the white man for that which he has. We are not in such condition as being at the mercy of the white race, as long as we are members of the Asiatic Nation.

AMERICA WILL DESTROY HERSELF

2-15-62

A Messenger or a Prophet of God is always sent to a people to warn them of the time. He is a Warner of some great and dreadful event to take place upon the earth's inhabitants for their wrong-doings and idol worshipping.

The Messenger's job was always to separate the people he was sent to from the evil doers, lest they all be destroyed. In the previous histories, according to the Bible and Holy Qur'an, Allah sent Noah to his people to warn them and teach them of Allah's wrath soon to be brought down on them for their inequities and idol worshipping. If they did not submit to His teachings and separate from the ones who were leading the people from Allah, they were overtaken by destruction.

The Independent One

Allah desires that His people to be obedient to Him. he does not need us, as He is the Independent One and is able to stand alone. We are dependent upon Him.

Abraham was also raised to deliver his people and warn them of Allah's anger and His promise of death if they did not submit to Allah and separate from the one who rejected Him.

Moses was another Warner to his people to bring them into the knowledge of Allah and a death penalty if they did not submit to Him.

These histories serve as a sign to you today. It serves to make you see that if you do not submit to Allah, His wrath will most surely be brought down on you.

Signs and Warnings

These histories are signs and warnings to white America of what comes to nations that stand in the way, oppose Allah's message and mislead the very people to whom the message is sent.

Were not the people who rejected Noah and make mock of the believers destroyed? Abraham had to separate his people from the idol worshippers and all who refuse to separate were destroyed.

Were not the people destroyed who rejected Lot's warnings? What do you think Allah will do to the people today who reject his Last Messenger and will not separate from their enemy?

A Plain Understanding of The Red Dragon

Allah's Last Messenger

Allah has sent me as His last Messenger. I am a Warner to my people, the so-called Negroes, to separate themselves from the slave-master. Compare these different histories, prophets and their messages to that I am teaching my people, the so-called Negroes today.

I am also teaching you of Allah's anger directed to the slave master for his great sins and misleading the so-called Negro who is sacred in the eyes of Allah.

All those who did not separate themselves from the evil doers in Noah's time were destroyed. I am teaching you the same thing today.

My people, separate yourselves from the enemy or burn in their prepared hell fire. Their fair-play shown to you today is only to deceive you. They desire to take as many of you to hell with them as possible. Mr. preacher, I do not want to take your congregation from you, I only want to teach them the truth (Islam) and the consequences they must pay if they will not listen.

By nature we the Aboriginals are superior. We are not of the grafted race of white devils. We are the first and the last. They (the enemy) are those whom Jesus made mention of as being devils and by nature haters and murderers of the black nation. There can be no change in them unless you re-graft them and time is too precious to waste time re-grafting an evil people to good.

Their time is up on our planet. Today they are seeking ways to remain on the earth. They are by nature haters of Allah, the God of truth and justice, and have opposed Him and the righteous ever since being on our planet.

I am Allah's last Messenger and have been missioned to you (so- called Negroes). Come to Islam and escape the hell fire that has been prepared for the enemy of God and all those who follow after him. I am not of myself, for Allah has sent me to deliver you. Do not let them trick you to their death.

THE DEVIL IN DISGUISE

4-26-62

Disguise: That which is under disguise; a false or misleading appearance, used to hide who one really is, make a person look like someone else, deception, concealment, unfriendly opponent.

The first work of God on His coming was to make manifest to the world His and the Righteous One's enemies. The chief enemy of the Black, Brown, Yellow and Red man is the devil, the man of sin; created or rather grafted from the black man into a distinct, independent being. He was made an unlike, thus, enabling him to attract the alike. So said Allah (God) to me - unlike attracts and alike repels. The devils, being endowed with the knowledge of both good and evil could, therefore, with such knowledge and power of attraction, appear as he is or like a righteous person, as a friend or a sincere adviser. (Holy Qur'an 7:21)

Misled Original People

The devils, white race, have misled the whole of the original people of the earth. The devils are not original, they are a new race made six thousand years ago, as Allah has taught me. Read the Bible; Rev. 12:9: "And the great dragon was cast out, that old serpent called the Devil and Satan which deceiveth the whole world." And Allah said to me that we allowed them to be created to try them at ruling the righteous until the righteous produced one Supreme in wisdom and power Who by His Word or Will is capable of bringing about that which He pleases. This is He Who teaches me all that I know. He is the Great Champion of our faith, Islam, Whose rule will be truth, justice and righteousness.

Evil Injustice In Rule

The devils have ruled the nations under evil and injustice; this Mighty One's rule will be righteous. We must come into the knowledge of our next ruler! But how can we appreciate or recognize a Ruler or God of righteousness, until we first have a thorough knowledge of the present ruler of evil and unrighteousness? You must know the truth of this pale face, blue-eyed, race of devils, who have deceived you and our fathers. The entire history of them is written in evil and bloodshed. They have shed your blood like water; yet, you love them. Your love for them will surely get you hell! The

Bible and Holy Qur'an warns you and me against taking them for friends.

Fear Governs Acts

Of course, your fear of them makes you act, say and do things you would not if the fear had not been present. Accept Allah, the True God, and His religion, Islam, and He will remove the fear of them from you. They were created and made to be our enemies and also they were made to be destroyed by fire. You cannot reform them (devils) unless you graft them back into who they came from, the Black Nation, as Allah taught me, to Whom be praised forever.

They lead or invite you to nothing but evil, filth, sport and play. And they make you believe that they are God's chosen people to lead and guide you on the right way; that is, the head of the church, Pope, whom the Christians call, the "father" and vice regent of God.

In the church of the devil's religion is where he disguises himself as a Divine Guide. The Catholics are the chiefs of the Christian religion and are out to deceive the so-called Negroes in America to keep them from going over to the true religion of ISLAM.

The devils in Christianity are stripping their followers of their clothes. The women wearing their dresses above the knees, one of the most indecent things a woman could do: walk or ride in the public dressed half-nude.

'Divine Chastisement for Any Man Who Worships the Beast, The Human Serpent'

(Rev. 14:9-10) 4-11-59

FOR BEHOLD, I will send serpents, cockatrices among you, which will not be charmed and they shall bite you, saith the Lord." (Jer. 8:17)

The above said scripture is a warning to you and me against the love and worship of the devils, the human serpents. Here God promises the willful worshipers of his enemies, that He will even send those whom you take for friends above Him, against you, and make them bite you, do you evil. For believing and obeying the serpent, the devil, after knowledge of God and His religion, Adam and his wife were punished by the serpent, the devil: "And I will put enmity between thy seed and her seed. It shall bruise thy head and thou shalt bruise his heel," Gen. 5:15. God is not to be mocked. He warns us against loving and taking the devils for friends. Allah, alone, is our friend and most certainly is able to make us know it.

The black man has ever suffered from his mistake in taking the white race for his friends. From that incident in Eden, six thousand years ago to this day, there is enmity and hatred between the two people (black and white). This cannot be removed except by the removal of one or the other race. The two could never come to and live up to a just agreement to do justice between each other. It is the impossible, unless their nature is changed. Adam and his wife accepted the advice of the devil against their Lord, and the serpent, the devil, has misled and put to death the prophets and the righteous servants of God ever since the fall of Adam.

SERPENT

That old serpent, called the devil and Satan, which deceiveth the whole world (Rev. 12:9) is a person or persons whose characteristics are like that of a serpent (snake). Serpents or snakes of the grafted type cannot be trusted, for they will strike you when you are not expecting a strike.

Let us refer to Genesis: "Dan shall be a serpent by the way, an adder in the path that biteth the horse's heels so that his rider shall fall backward" (Gen. 49:17). Here Jacob on his deathbed foretelleth the future of his sons (Moses calls Dan a lion's whelp; he shall leap from Bashan; Deut. 33:22). That old serpent, devil and Satan, the old beast, is the dragon which deceiveth the whole world of the poor ignorant darker nations and has caused them to fall off their mount of prosperity, success and independence by accepting advice, guidance and empty promises which he (the serpent-like Caucasian devil) never intended to fulfill.

How well the prophets have described the characteristics of this race of devils as corresponding to the nature of a snake (serpent). Most snakes wobble and make a crooked trail when and wherever they crawl. So it is with the white race, which goes among the black nation leaving the marks of evil and crooked dealings and doings.

In spiritual dealings, there again you will find them like a snake (serpent), following on the heels of the truth bearers (prophets and messengers of God) to bite the believers with false teachings and fear in order that he may cause them to fall off their mount of truth. Like a snake (serpent) he parks in and on the pathway of all the so-called Negroes who seek the way to freedom, truth, justice and equality (Allah and the true religion, Islam). In many instances, they threaten you with imprisonment, the loss of your jobs, hunger, lack of shelter and disrespect of human rights. On some occasions, they threaten to take away your very life! By speaking evil of the truth (Allah and His apostle and Islam), they cause fear to enter the hearts of the weak believers and they fall off the mount of the truth of God which would have saved them from fear, harm, hunger and lack of shelter. As he caused the fall of Adam and his wife from the Garden of Paradise, so they are trying to cause the fall of you and me and prevent us from entering Paradise by not believing in Allah and His religion, Islam.

Allah (God) drove out both Adam and Eve and cursed the serpent and set a day of execution upon the (human) serpent (the devil and Satan) and enmity and hatred (discord, dislike, disapproval) between the apostles and prophets of God and the human serpent. "And God said unto the serpent, because thou hast done this, thou art cursed above all cattle, and above every beast of the field, and I will put enmity between thee and the woman and between thy seed and her seed, it shall bruise thy head and thou shall bruise his heel" (Gen. 3:15).

Notice that the above verse refers to the woman's seed as "it" and in the last two words of verse 15, "his heel" is used. The woman's seed and the serpent's seed are involved. Therefore, the seed of the two will settle the wrong between the woman and the serpent caused by the serpent in the Garden of Paradise 6,000 years ago. The woman's seed shall bruise the serpent's head.

What is the head of this human serpent? It is the false religious leaders of the human beast serpent. "Come hither, I will show unto thee the judgment of the great whore that sitteth upon many waters with whom kings of the earth have committed fornication and the inhabitant's of the earth have been made drunk." (They are silly drunk from the false religious teachings of the head of the serpent. Under this drunkenness they war against the truth and persecute and kill the servants of truth, thinking that they are doing God's will, or they try to prevent the truth from manifesting falsehood).

In the fourth verse, the woman is arrayed in purple and scarlet color and is filthy. In the first and sixteenth verses, she is called a whore. The beast supports her.

THE BEAST PART I

Who is like unto the beast? Who is able to make war with him?" (Rev. 13:4). This beast that is spoken of in the prophecy of the first book of the Bible called Revelations and has and still is being much misunderstood by my people. But one thing is certain, the name (beast) is believed by most all readers of the Book to refer to a person or persons, which is right. But who is the person or persons? (Note: There is mentioned in the same chapter and verse a dragon which gave power to the beast. Who can this dragon be? Is he also a person? Then how are the two related?)

The eighteenth verse of the same chapter reads: "Here is wisdom. Let him that hath understanding count the number of the beast: for it is the number of a man." Here we arc told that the number of the beast referred to here is a man or people. Now the only way of knowing just what man or people is to watch and see what man or people's doings or works compare with the doings and works of the symbolic beast of the Revelation.

This name "beast," when given to a person, refers to that person's characteristics, not to an actual beast. Study the history of how America treats the freedom, justice and equality which is supposed to be given to all citizens of America (of course the Negroes are not citizens of America). A citizen. cannot and will not allow his people and government to treat him in such way as America treats her so-called Negroes.

To call a person a "beast" is simply to say, according to the English language: Nouns—violent person, berserk or berserker, demon, fiend, shaitan or sheitan or Satan, or dragon, evil spirit, Satanas, devil, diable, Iblis, azazel, abaddon, apollyon, the prince of the devils, the prince of darkness, the prince of this world, the prince of the power of air, the wicked one, the evil one, the archenemy, the archfiend, the devil incarnate, the father of lies, the author and father of evil, the serpent, the common enemy, the angel of the bottomless pit. Adjectives— satanic, devilish, diabolic (al), hell-born, demoniac, savage, brute, fierce, vicious, wild, untamed, tameless, ungentle, barbarous, unmitigated, unsoftened, ungovernable, uncontrollable (obstinate), brute force, forcibly, by main, with might and main, by force of arms, at the point of the sword or bayonet (the devil and Satan). The above in the explanation of "beast" when applied to human beings or people in general, according to Roget's International Thesaurus. The so-called American Negroes have and still suffer under such brutish treatment from the American Christian white race, who call themselves followers of Jesus and his God.

The Revelator could not have better described the white race's way of dealing with the black nation. They (white race) are the people described as "beast" in the Revelation of the Bible. Study them and their history and dealings with people and you will without hesitation agree with me 100 per cent that these are the people meant by the Revelator, who foresaw their future and end and wrote it while he and his followers were in exile from the Holy Land 6,600 years ago on the Island of Pelan in the Aegean Sea, where he grafted the present white race.

The revelation is claimed by the Christians to have been given to a Saint John Divine who was a follower of Jesus, but this is erroneous and wrong. It is by the father of the white race (Mr. Yakub or Jacob). The people other than the beast are mentioned as worshipers of the beast: "And they (the people of the darker nation) worshipped the dragon which gave power unto the beast." The power given by the dragon to the beast refers to a higher wisdom and knowledge of the time and wise preparedness. The chief head and spiritual guidance of the white race is the Pope of Rome.

THE BEAST PART II

WHO IS ABLE TO MAKE WAR WITH HIM?

Who is able to make war with him? (Rev. 13:4) dreadful and terrible (Dan. 7:7).

God and His Prophets could not have given the white race a better name (serpent) according to the characteristics of that race. The serpent of Genesis 3:1 was none other than the devil (white race). He deceived Adam and his wife, causing them to disobey Allah (God), which was the plan of the serpent (devil), according to the history of the devils. Their greatest desire is to make the righteous disobey the law of righteousness.

They are referred to by this name "serpent" in the Holy Qur'an (37:65) translated by Maulvi Muhammad Ali: "To a tree that grows in the bottom of hell, its produce is as the heads of serpents which the disbelievers shall eat from." In his footnote (2112), he says: "That the Arabs apply the name Shaitan to a sort of serpent having a mane, ugly or foul in the head and face." In Mr. Abdullah Yusuf Ali's translation of the Holy Qur'an in English, the same chapter and verse (37:65), it reads: "The shoots of its fruit stalks are like the heads of devils."

The Bible's forbidden tree (Gen. 2:17) was a tree of the knowledge of good and evil. This also tells us that the tree was person, for trees know nothing! This tree of knowledge was forbidden to Adam and Eve. The only one whom this tree could be is the devil. After deceiving Adam and his wife, he has been called a serpent due to his keen knowledge of tricks and his acts of shrewdness; he made his acquaintance with Adam and his wife in the absence of God. Since this is the nature of a liar, he can best lie to the people when truth is absent.

We know that there was never a time when an actual serpent (or snake) could talk and deceive people in the knowledge of God's law. This same serpent is mentioned in Revelation 12: 9 as a deceiver. There (12:9) it is made clear to us that the serpent is "the dragon, devil and Satan which deceiveth the whole world." In Gen. (3:1) he appeared in the Garden of Paradise before the woman and deceived her (Rev. 12:4). He stood before the woman who was ready to be delivered to devour her child as soon as it is born.

The serpent, the devil, dragon, Satan, seems to have been seeking the weaker part of man (the woman) to bring to naught the man—the Divine Man. It is his first and last trick to deceive the people of God through the woman or with the woman. He is using his woman to tempt the black man by parading her half-nude before his eyes and with public love-making, indecent kissing and dancing over radio and television screens and throughout their public papers and magazines. He is flooding the world with propaganda against God and His true religion, Islam. He stands before the so-called Negro woman to deceive her by feigning love and love-making with her, give the so-called Negro woman preference over her husband or brother in hiring.

In some cities, the Negro woman receives a much higher salary that the so-called Negro man. The devil takes the so-called Negro woman and puts his hands and arms around her body. She may be married or single, it makes no difference. Whenever he can he is making eyes at her. This is an outright destruction of the moral principles of the black man.

In some cities, we convert five to one woman. The so-called Negroes should unite and put a stop to the destruction of their women by the serpent. The woman in (Rev. 12:4) actually refers to the last Apostle of God, and her child refers to his followers, or the entire Negro race as they are called, who are not ready to be delivered (go to their own).

"THE SERPENT BITE" - To cause trouble, disappointment, imprisonment, the loss of a good friend, the loss of paradise, the hereafter, to cause sickness and death. They did bite the disobedient followers of Moses (Numbers 21:6). Regardless of your good intentions for the serpent, he will bite you just the same. Who is any more submissive and lovable to the white man than the Originals (so-called Negroes)? Yet they receive the worst treatment from the whites than all the others of his kind. A couple of weeks ago I was told a few devils in Texas lynched a black man right on the streets for just disputing the devil's word. I know of plenty of places in the South where you will be killed if you dispute a devil's word or even ask for justice. I was born in such a place, and his Northern brothers are not angels to you and me; so, do not feel safe anywhere unless you are a believer in Allah.

AS IT IS WRITTEN of us: "They lived their life long under the very shadow of death." The Originals (so-called Negroes) are now offered the sure friendship of Allah (God), but they prefer the friendship of the devils, the serpent, rather than

God. They are being beaten and murdered daily by them and denied justice everywhere. There just is no justice for us under this kind of people.

Allah (God) desired that we come to the knowledge of Him and His salvation, which he holds for us; therefore, the Holy Qur'an teaches us that he will send the devils against the disbelievers. Since it is the devils whom you believe in, then by the devils you should learn from their actions and treatment that they are the devils.

ALLAH IS WELL able to prove His word true. The serpent cannot bite true Muslims, they are forbidden to him. The cockatrice mentioned in the chapter is just another name of the devils, which means: a monster, reptile, evil eye, a deceiver. So fly to Allah and keep away from the bite of the serpent.

Everything Has Failed

Islam comes after everything fails. It's significance is the making of Peace. The Muslims' greeting to each other is. "Peace." What better religion could we desire after being divided, and made enemies of each other? Don't tell us that you have "unity and peace" in the white race's religion called Christianity. The white race does not like Islam, because it is truth: entire submission to the will of Allah. This is against their nature. They can't live the life of Freedom, Justice and Equality, not even among themselves.

Many of you sing that old song, "Give me that old time religion." Islam is that "old time religion." It is as old as God Himself, and God is the Author of Islam. Islam was not invented as in the case of Christianity and other religions. Islam came with Allah (God) and the Universe. The Holy Qur'an says: "This day I have perfected for you, your religion and completed my favor on you; and have chosen for you, Islam as a religion." (5:3)

Here, Islam claims to be a perfect religion, and its Author, the Perfect One is God. What can be imperfect about Islam when it means, "entire submission to the Will of God?" What can be wrong or imperfect about this religion, Islam, which was the religion of Noah, Abraham, Moses, Jesus, and all the Prophets of God, to Muhammad, the last of the Prophets? Islam proves that it's Author is God; inasmuch as Allah (God) is on the side of every True Muslim. This is easy to see today.

Every one of you who are accepting Islam in America, can bear me witness that for the first time in your life, you feel the power and help of Almighty Allah (God) on your side. Your whole life becomes a change for the better. Your fear is removed; your grief is gone. Your desire to continue doing evil things is leaving you for good. Love for your brother (your people) for the first time is now becoming a reality. It is the Aim of Allah (God), in giving to you and I, Islam, to unite us and to remove fear, sorrow, and sickness and bring us into that heavenly life, peace of mind, and contentment.

Do you mean to say that you don't need such religion? Or, do you say that the white race-made Christianity is giving you peace and contentment, whose world-recognized father is the Pope of Rome, not Jesus, nor Allah (God), it is the father of the Christian religion, as practiced by the white race, and those who believe in it.

Islam is universally recognized as being the true religion of the Divine Supreme Being. The proof that it is the true religion of God, and that it will get power and friendship for you, with Allah (God) and the Righteous: Why is the Federal Government and its thousands of agents doing everything in their power, except outright shooting you, to keep you from believing in Allah and His True Religion, Islam? They are trying, and tricking you in many ways, under the false disguise as now being a friend of yours and wanting you to forget the past, but your agreement with them will not stand when you see the showdown.

Islam is the natural religion of the Black Nation. The nature in which they are made, and we are called to return to Islam in these words from the Holy Qur'an: "Set your face upright for religion in the right state. The nature made by Allah in which he has made men: There is no altering of Allah's Creation: That is the right religion, but most people do not know."

The devils know the true religion of Allah, and have always known it, but they will not teach it, because it is against their nature to believe and teach the true religion of God, which would upset their chances of ruling the people under falsehood. WHY NOT ISLAM?

ALLAH OFFERS YOU A FUTURE

You and I, the so-called American Negroes, are helpless without Allah (God) and Islam, which is the religion of God, His prophets, and our people. We are at the mercy of the Christian World. What has the Christian World done for you and me? Why should we want to remain in it? Have not they continued to segregate you, line you up and burn you, don't they continue to beat your heads and your brains, burst out your ears and eyes? They have done these things to us. They did these things even as you called yourself a Christian. They have shown that they don't recognize you as their equal. Why don't you exercise that freedom which they offer you and go back to your own?

If our share of this earth is not in this Western Hemisphere, then we must look for it in the East. However, 25,000,000 so-called Negroes who have been lost from their own people for 400 years must have a home on this earth that they can call their own. Allah, the Great God of the Universe, will give us the whole earth if we submit to Him and have patience to wait on Him. Regardless of the cost, we must have some earth of our own. Let not the false show and promises of this world deceive you so that you be the loser.

You make yourself a despised people in the eyes of the civilized world by hating yourself and loving the enemy, devil. The Original man, Allah has declared, is none other than the Blackman. He is the first and last, maker and owner of the Universe. The brown, yellow, red and white, all came from the Blackman. The Blackman used a special method of birth control law to produce the white race.

The true knowledge of black and white mankind should be enough to awaken the so-called Negroes, put them on their feet and on the road to self independence. You my people are so afraid of the slave-master, that you even love them to the point of your own destruction. You wish the bearer of truth would not tell the truth, even if he knows it. You hate a leader that tries to unite you to your own kind. Allah offers you a future, an eternal future. This world has no future. It was doomed when it was created. I speak and write what has been given to me from Allah (God), to Whom praise is due. I am not here to excite you for wealth or praise. I don't want your wealth. I don't want your praise. I want for you the thing which will produce unity of self and our kind. I want you safe. The world knows that I want you safe. What I preach is for our own life and the life of our children.

It is Allah's will and purpose that we shall know ourselves. He came Himself to teach us the knowledge of self. How else may you account for the success of my followers and myself? Who is better knowing of who we are than God Himself? All praise is due to the Great Mahdi (Allah in Person), Who was to come and has come. He is the Sole Master of the Worlds. I ask myself at times, "What can I do to repay Allah, the Great Mahdi, Fard Muhammad, for His coming, wisdom, knowledge and understanding?

My followers and I have and are still spending much time and money to awaken our people to the knowledge of self. We are suffering much persecution and ridicule to awaken our people to the knowledge of their own salvation. our present suffering is nothing compared to the joy that awaits us as a people united for one common cause serving Allah, The God of Abraham, Moses, Jesus and our forefathers. Allah has declared that we must know ourselves and unite onto our own kind or suffer the consequences. The new government controlled by the Roman Catholics, will stop at nothing in their effort to win the black people of

America to them, but the Negroes must know that this world's end is near.

IF ANY MAN WORSHIP THE BEAST AND HIS IMAGE

(Rev. 14:9, 10) 4-4-59

WE ARE warned in the plainest words against the love and worship of the symbolic beast (the Caucasian race) and not even to receive his mark in our heads or hands. To do so will bring upon us the wrath of God without mercy, according to the 10th verse of the above Chapter 1. There are no darker people on earth who worship this race of people as the American so-called Negroes do. Due to the lack of knowledge of this race and their fear of them, they ignorantly love and admire them, their open enemies, who are the enemies of God and His prophets. While you faithfully pray to God that you may not be a follower of the devils, you even now love and worship them. Come out of them and save yourselves from the wrath of Almighty Allah (God).

INTEGRATION will not solve our problem in this late day and time of the judgement of the white race. Your problem can only be solved by your separation from the white race. This will be brought about by the work of God. Your names are of the beasts' (white race's) names. Your religion and God, language and everything, are of the white race. To escape their doom and the wrath of God, you are warned to come out of them.

"The mark in the forehead or in his hand," refers to your face or hands. It is the face which includes the eyes, mouth, nose and forefront. It is in the face where one looks for a sign of what the person really is. If the sign is not in his or her general expression, it is in the eyes or what comes out of the mouth in words. The hand is marked by the work they do in favor of the beast, which comes from the head of our bodies. Therefore, whatever is in us, the mark or sign is in our forehead or the work of our hands. Those who love the devils (the beast) are known by their works, looks, talk, actions, and guilt.

THE WORKS of the beast are evil and filth, sport and play, games of chance, love songs and temptation, drunkenness, murder and robbery. Under the above, they captivate you (the so-called Negroes).

You need plenty of teaching along these lines of how to keep yourselves from being marked by the devils as unbelievers in your God. Remember, you were reared by the devils, and your flesh and blood are already marked by them. Today, they (the devils) are like roaring lions among you after your girls and women, and many of his women and girls are after you for the sole purpose of marking you as unfit to see the hereafter. God allows the devils to tempt you that you may receive the infidel mark of unbelief in God, but He will surely punish you who receive such mark.

The poor Negro preachers who understand not the scripture, nor God and the devil, preach that you should love everybody, which includes the devils, while God forbids us to love His or our own enemies, not to mention the arch-enemy devil. I warn you to receive not the mark of the beast in your head or hand.

Mr. Muhammad Speaks On The Negroes' Salvation

"The Lost and Found Must Be Restored"

White America is in great fear of the rise of her sleeping, mentally dead slaves, the lost found members of the Black Nation of Asia. The lost sheep, the Bible's symbolic lost sheep (Matt. 12:11; 18:12) is now found after having been kidnapped by the thieving wolf, and held a prey by the power of the Beast in the wilderness (Dan. 7:7, Rev. 18:4, Isaiah 49: 24: 25). The finding of the lost members of the great Asiatic Black Nation means the end of the world that you and I have known. These truths are of the utmost importance to the future of the so-called Negroes, although they have no knowledge of their importance.

The so-called Negroes must be separated from the white race and given a home on this earth that they can call their own. The prophetic 400 years of slave service for the slave-masters in a country that is not their own (Gen. 15:13; 14) and the history of the lost and found members (the so-called Negroes) of the Original Black Nation begins in the Bible's first book called Genesis, and ends in the last book called Revelations (Rev. 14:19; and 20). There are no parables in the Bible more fitting to our history here in America, than the parable of the "Lost Sheep," and "The Prodigal Son" (St Luke 15:1; 8; 11). These parables show the great love and joy for the Finder (God, in the person of Master Fard Muhammad) Who, in the year 1930 to 1933 made known that he had found us, and immediately began preparing for our return.

The return of the lost-found, so-called Negroes, to their own people and country, raises and completes all of [what the prophetic Bible] teachers are said to be prophecy. It also closes the present Holy Qur'an which was revealed after the Torah and Gospel, whose message is directed at giving the necessary qualifications for the return of the lost-found, which are absent in the Bible. With out saying it, the Holy Qur'an, whose Author and Teacher is God Himself, is unlike the Bible, whose authors and teachers are said to be prophets, historians, theologians, who were sent from God.

The Holy Qur'an was revealed at the right time and place. It is called "Al-Hudd" or "The Guidance" (2:2). "Al-Furqan" or "That which makes a distinction between truth and falsehood" (15:1). It is also called "An-Nur" or "The Light" (7:157). Divine light, right guidance, and the truth that will show up the false teachings under which the found Negroes have been reared, are the first and the last necessary steps toward a return to your own. This truth is now causing much annoying talk, false charges and threats of death for the bearer of truth, to the so-called Negroes (my people). They, the Negroes, must know the truth. They must be separated and joined again to their own people. This will be done unless you are able to make God and His Prophets liars, and this you cannot do, even with the aid of all the devils.

Symbolically, the Negroes are the absent sheep of the one hundred, and the tenth piece of silver that demanded the sweeping of the house, the Nations, in order to find it. They are also the Prodigal Son who was lost, dead and alive, requiring that the father go after him in order to find him.

MR. MUHAMMAD SPEAKS

"Say to those who believe that they forgive those who do not fear the Days of Allah, that He may reward a people for what they earn." (Holy Qur'an 45:14)

What is meant by "Days of Allah (God)" are the battles between right and wrong. They are often mentioned as follows: the Days of Judgement, the days of the Resurrection, the Days of the Son of Man, and the Days of Allah (God). These days must not be mistaken for the regular twenty-four hour day. NO, the Days of Allah, the Days of the Resurrection, the Days of Judgement, and the Days of the Son of Man mean years; not the common twenty-four hour day.

What will make us know when we are living in the Days of Allah (God)? It is by the fulfilling of the predictions made by the Prophets of Allah (God), long before they come to pass. I quote. Maulvi Muhammad Ali's foot note 2276 on this verse, in which he says: "The Days of Allah are the contests in which the righteous shall be made successful." That, no one can deny; for this is a sign for the disbelievers who have enjoyed great temporary prosperity; and who thought that they were too rich and powerful to be brought into a state of helplessness. Although they had the histories of those who were before them, there is no difference between the disbelievers - today or the past.

We are living in the Days of Allah (God); the earth and its people have been ruled by the evil race known as the white race. In these Days of Allah (God), the righteous (the Muslims) are now gaining power over the wicked, and will soon rule the earth again as they did before the creation of the white race.

Take notice of my followers (the so-called Negroes) who have given up the wicked ways of the white race and their self-styled Christianity, and have accepted the Truth (the religion of Islam). They are gradually becoming the most successful people in the world. Allah has chosen us, we have chosen Allah.

Who can successfully oppose Allah (God) in His Days and time of rule? It is easy to give up a weak and poverty stricken people, but it is not so easy when they are powerful and wealthy. They think there will be no end to their power and wealth which is made to deceive them.

NO JUSTICE FOR US IN USA

We have wondered why white people hate and mistreat us after we have been so obedient, so submissive, with "hat in hand" and a scared smile or grin on our faces from ear to ear.

We have killed their enemies for them, and sometimes those whom they called their enemies were our own people. For 400 years, we've tried to understand why the white race here in America hate, beat and kill their helpless free slaves, and yet preach Jesus Christ and God's love and justice; but even those white preachers and priests, the Pope (Father of the Church) have never united and protested to the government against the lawless, out- right beating and killing of us, the so-called American Negroes. (Members of the Tribe of Shabazz).

INJUSTICE INCREASED

Even today, while the government is offering integration, (which will not solve our problem, but make it harder to solve) injustice to us have increased!

And the so-called `God-sent' white and black preachers of Christianity are not using their churches and followers to protest against these injustices. We are witnesses them, into a lake of fire. (The lake is none other than the entire continent of North against them, even by the recent police brutality and murder of our people in Los Angeles, April 27, 1962.

We do not have united Christian preachers nor priests of the churches protesting against such unprovoked, lawless, outright murder of our people. Even, according to the Los Angeles Times and the Herald-Examiner newspapers, the black preachers spoke in sympathy with that ungodly, merciless, brute police force headed by the worst hater (William Parker) of the black people in this unjust government of America. Today, Allah is making them manifest to the world as a race of devils, made to be our enemies and murderers until the day of their doom (which is very near).

HITS `FREE DEVIL MURDERS'

Here in North America will the fire of hell take place first on those who sit and rejoice to see poor, innocent black men burned to ashes, at the hands of the free devil murderers of our people.

The black people of America must be given the knowledge of self and of these open heartless devils whose aims today are to take the poor black people to hell with them, while at the same time give you as much death and hell at their hands before Allah takes them into a lake of fire. (The lake is none other than the entire continent of North America).

They teach love, but this does not mean that they love you because of your belief in Christianity. NO! But rather that you love them - this will make you an enemy of God. I have warned you the white race's name alone will get you hell from God. they would like that you believe as you have always in that which they taught you - Christianity!

They call the Truth that I have received from Allah "hate teachings" because it makes them manifest. Who could love the devils after having the knowledge of them?

DELIVER POOR AND NEEDY

Read the following chapters and verses from your Bible which refers to you and them: Psalms 82:3,4. "Do justice to the afflicted; deliver the poor and needy; rid them out of the hands of the wicked (the white devils of the U.S.A.) They (the black people of America) know not, neither will they understand, they walk on into darkness.

All the foundation of the earth is out of course. (Not the earth itself, but the governments of the wicked is out of a wise course.) Justice standeth afar off (for the so-called Negroes.) Truth is fallen in the streets (is not accepted.)

"None calleth for justice (when it is for so-called Negroes, nor any pleadeth for the Truth; (They trust the devil's lies) the devils feet run to do evil, they make haste to shed innocent blood. (Kill a so-called Negro.) Their thoughts are evil, wasting and destruction." (Isa. 59:4,9,14

Let us unite and seek some of this good earth for a home that we can call our own! Leave a people who are daily bent upon your destruction, your disgrace and shame alone!

PEACE?

Can there be any peace for the peace-breaker? Allah told me that six thousand years ago, this same people's fathers (white race) broke the peace of the righteous in the gardens of Eden (the place that is known as old Persia). They called the truth of God a lie and made lies the truth.

They said to the people of the Garden, according to the Bible (Gen. 3:4-6), "And the serpent (a name used according to the evil, deceiving characteristics of the Caucasian race) said unto the woman, you shall not surely die; for God doth know that in the day you eat thereof, then your eyes shall be opened, and you shall be as gods..." The serpent lied, because they did die. And the deceiver (serpent) was driven out of the garden into the wilderness of the earth to build a wicked kingdom of evil to be destroyed on the coming of God.

They (the white race) are playing the same trick on the black nation today as they die in the days of Adam. They shall suffer eternal expulsion from this earth in a lake of fire (Rev. 20:10). Can they enjoy peace? After they were cast out of the garden, according to the Holy Qur'an; 7:16, "because thou hast thrown me out of the way, Lo, I will lie in wait for them on the straight way." As he had deceived Adam and his wife, he now declares that he will deceive the righteous in their straight path in the days of the resurrection and judgement of his evil world. He swore to them in another place that he would lead them to a tree of immorality and a kingdom that decays not. This kind of teaching is found in the teachings of Christianity. It is a very clever way of deceiving the black people of America, for here, Satan represents himself as an angel of light. They paint a picture of lies of "beyond the grave," when they know there is no life or communication with the dead. All ceases to be life after death. This is universally known.

Can they have peace? When they were created to destroy the peace of the righteous, as it is written, "Destruction cometh; and they shall seek peace, and there shall be none, mischief shall come upon mischief and rumor shall be upon rumor," (Ezekiel 7:25). They wrongfully represent themselves as peacemakers and lovers of peace and freedom (but only for themselves). This kind of talk deceives the nations while at the same time they are the troublemakers. As it is written; "but the wicked are like the troubled sea when it cannot rest, whose waters cast up mire and dirt." So it is with this wicked race, whom God has permitted to become the richest and most progressed people of earth. The more they increase in riches and power, the more they seek to trouble those that are at peace with them. They envy the peace and progress of others and are never satisfied, though they have the world bowing at their feet. They are forever deceiving the poor so-called Negroes with false promises and the so-called Negroes seem to love it. There is no peace for the wicked saith the God of peace (Isa. 57;20,21) The only peace today is with Allah and in His religion of peace, Islam. Believe it or leave it! Hurry and join onto your own kind. The time of this world is at hand.

THE DEVILS GOING RAMPANT

5-16-59

THE ADAM's (devil) children, the great trouble-makers, the demon, the fiend, Shaitan, the Adam's human beasts, the hell-raisers, the open arch-enemies of God, and all black mankind, who in the beginning disobeyed the law of God and introduced evil, filth and disrespect for God and His law of justice and righteousness among the nation of righteous (the black, brown, yellow and red people) are now on their traditional rampage against us, the so-called Negroes (their good old 400-year old slaves).

They have been murdering and raping us throughout the centuries and yet you are foolish enough to love and adore them (the devils) after all of their evils poured upon you and me. It just does not make sense.

Do not be surprised at anything like evil that you see them do; only be surprise when you see them do an act of good in your favor. Evil is the nature of Adam's children. They even have you believing that you are from Adam which is absolutely false.

Never say that you are from Adam. Adam was the father (devil) of sin and disobedience, the devil of you and me.

THE RECENT Parker lynching and the Florida rape of one of our girls, who was gagged and tied by four devils taking turns one after the other on her last Saturday morning (May 2) outside of the capital city of Florida (Tallahassee), a savage beast could not do worse. They swooped down upon two of our original girls like hungry wolves after lambs with drawn shot guns and knives to destroy the virginity of our daughters and kill their black boyfriends if they attempted to try to protect the girls.

Of Course, the boys would have been given more credit if they had received death in trying to defend their women against the filthy devils' attack. What good is our lives to us to allow our enemies to come into our families and rape our wives and daughters and lynch our men at will? Unite on the side of Allah and He will help us to put a stop to it, or die trying in the name of Allah.

APPEALING FOR justice from the lynchers and rapists brothers will avail us nothing. Parker's Mississippi mob of devils, the law's excuse is that the murderers cannot be found. The sheriff knew that Parker was charged with rape. Why did not he try to protect his prisoner by keeping the jail well guarded from an attempt by his lynchers? How did the lynchers know where the keys were? Why did the nurse wait until the outlaws (lynchers) had captured their prey and was out of the town before notifying the sheriff's office or his home of the cries that she heard coming from the mouth of the murdered prisoner in and out of the jail? If it had been Negroes trying to take a white man out to lynch him, it would have been known at once; even to the U.S. Army!

Florida will protect her four devil rapists. She is already preparing a defense for them now by claiming the four devils to have been drunk, which we all know will be false. There is no justice for you under the American flag from their Supreme Courts to the jailhouse kangaroo courts. You fear to accept Allah and His true religion, Islam (Peace), and you will continue to suffer disgrace, beatings and killings at the hands of these devils. Remember, we live in a lawless world.

SEPARATION IS A MUST

The poor so-called Negroes (the lost found people of the black nation from the Tribe of Shabazz) in America, brought here by the white man in 1555; said Allah (God in person) the best Knower that our fathers and mothers were brought in chains at a great loss of life. According to history, we have served them (our slave masters) well for the past four hundred years. According to the Bible's history made by Abraham on receiving the prophecy of our enslavement in a strange land and people to serve for four hundred years.

America was not known to the white Europeans before Columbus discovery of the Western Hemisphere in 1492, four hundred and seventy years ago. Beyond a shadow of doubt, this is the strange land, and the white race, a strange people to the original Indians and our father, who were brought here in 1555, four hundred and seven years ago, did not know either the people (white and Indian) or the country, all were strangers.

If this is not the answer to Abraham's prophecy, then you may tell me. Today our unrest and longing for unity and love of self and kind, and the desire for freedom, justice, and equality, a home on this earth that we can call our own, and the presence of God among us, the giving and calling us after Divine names, is a true sign that we are the people that Abraham saw and prophesied that would be lost and must be found. The prophecy is mentioned in many places throughout the Bible. It ends with the struggle between the symbolic lamb and beast over the delivering of the same people (the so-called Negroes in America) from a wicked merciless murderer like a savage beast over a prey.

It is a must that we be separated from our Slave Master's children, who like their fathers, hate and despise us with murder and slavery in their hearts for us day and night. It is foolish and ignorant to hear any black man or woman praising the offer of integration with a four-hundred-year old enemy of ours, which is inviting death and destruction of both races. Not one offer to give the once slave land to build a government and nation of their own, where they can live without fear of being beaten and killed without justice. Our enemies go in gangs to kill you. They rejoice to do you harm, this you know.

They are not like you and me. Their father was a devil, who created them to be enemies of the black people (the righteous) by the spirit of their father (which was false and murderous) so are they, and today they are deceiving you under false pretenses that they will do good by you just to keep you here with them to share hell fire with them. My Allah will give us heaven if you will only believe and come follow me. we need a country to ourselves like all other nations, and we will get it soon. "Separate, whereof ye can come out from among them and be ye separate, saith the Lord, and touch not the unclean (the wicked white race) and I will receive you and will be a father unto you, and you shall be my sons and daughters, saith the Lord, Almighty (2 Chor 6:17,18)" And I heard another voice from heaven saying, Come out of her, my people that you be not partakers of her sins and that you receive not of her plagues. Rev.18.4

The Danger of Taking Enemies for Friends 6-6-59

"O, you who believe, do not take for intimate friends from among others than your own people; they do not fall short of inflicting loss upon you; they love what distresses you; vehement hatred has already appeared from out of their mouths, and what their hearts conceal is greater still. Indeed, we have made the communication clear to you if you will understand." (3:117).

WE, THE LOST and found members of the tribe of Shabazz (so-called Negroes), have for 400 years sought the friendship of our enemies - the white race, "the devils" - to the destruction of our own nation. The white race does not desire sincere friendship with black people. They may pretend to be your friends if you have something that they want, such as your women. Through her they corrupt your nation and bring it to disgrace before the nations of the earth, as they have done for the poor black people of America. Because of disunity among us and no control over our women, we stand by with folded arms, cowards to the core, and allow the human brute beast to take our women and little girls out of our arms, to beat, rape, and destroy the most priceless gift of a nation (its woman). We cannot produce a pure, chaste nation with a "free-for-all" woman. If we are too cowardly to protect her against the human beast's advances, we should kill ourselves and our women. This suicide of the race would get us more credit in the eyes of the civilized nations of the earth than for us to continue to allow our girls and women to be corrupted by this human beast.

WE DO NOT love our girls and woman as we should. If we did, we would protect them as other nations do. We should compel all of our males under the oath of death, regardless of faith, to regain control and protect our black girls and women from being corrupted by both our enemies and non-enemies. The white race has made us to respect him and his women; now let us make them and all races respect us and our women. First, by self-respect. Second, with the help of Allah and our lives.

We and friends to everyone but self and kind. Our enemies love what distresses us; but we are like the next verse says that we are: "Lo, you are they who will love them while they do not love you." (3:118).

Allah, to Whom all praises are due, said that: "You love the devils because they give you nothing." That is so true. They lynch, burn, rape, beat and kill you; yet you love and want to be like them in every way. Their way of life will get you and me hell fire, for they were created for hell fire and know it. But, their greatest desires is to carry you with them.

MAN GOES TO hell or heaven in this life, and to the grave or earth after death. To love the devils is to be one of them and an enemy of God. There is a Bible teaching that: "God so loved the world (the Negroes) that He gave His only begotten Son that through Him (the Son) that they may have eternal life." This is misunderstood. Allah (God) has never and never will give a prophet's (a son's) life to save the world of devils. That scripture refers to the so-called Negroes, who were born and reared up in the devil's world, who must now be redeemed by the God of Righteous (the promised Mahdi) or one whom He will choose from among the so-called Negroes to be His apostle (Messenger). This man is the one the scripture refers to as the first begotten of the dead mentally dead so-called Negroes). He is also the first born of God because his first birth and teaching was of the devils, which is considered a dead race without eternal life, for the life of the devil race was limited to 6,000 years.

So, the scripture makes a distinction between the races, or race and nation (black and white) by calling one (the devils) the dead or wicked, and the other (the original black nation), the people of eternal life; for the black nations have no limitation of life on the earth.

The Truth Has Come

5-2-59

"Say: The truth has come and the falsehood shall vanish. It neither creates nor reproduces anything new, nor restores anything; it shall not come back." (Holy Qur'an 34:49.)

WHAT has falsehood created or produced in the heaven and earth? We are now living in the time of truth, and falsehood cannot survive in the light of truth any more than darkness can survive in the presence of light. Allah has revealed the truth to me, and I am teaching it to you, but you do note believe it because of your love an fear of the slave-masters. They too will be made to lick the dust, by the power of Allah. There never has been an enemy of His that He lacked power to rid Himself of. Neither does Allah lack power to rid Himself and the Nation of Islam of this enemy that you fear and love; though you are even disgraced, beaten and killed by them, from your ministers of their slavery religion (Christianity) down to the lowly, ignorant man in the mud.

YOU HAVE MADE yourselves the most foolish people on the earth by loving and following after the ways of slave masters, whom Allah has revealed to me to be non other than real devils, and that their so-called Christianity is not His religion, nor the religion of Jesus or any other Prophet of Allah (God). You are a hard-headed, stiff-necked, rebellious people who are proud of your enemies and their slavery religion.

Allah is now sending the devils against you, that you may learn that His word is true, that they are heartless. Although they may do me and my followers evil, but by my Allah, they will not able to get away with it; for every harm done to or against us will be returned doubly and tripled. Allah (God) is with me in person to bless you and me with right guidance and protection if we believe and rely on Him; otherwise, He can do us evil.

ALLAH (God) has not come to bring about love and peace between us and the devils (our slave-masters) but rather to separate and make manifest to you and me our open enemies, the enemies of God and His prophets. We are now living in the judgement of this evil world of the devils, and the separation of the Bible's symbolic goats and sheep is now in effect. How blind you are, unable to see the truth, though it is like sunshine.

Do you not see and hear how your people of Africa from whom you were taken 400 years ago are separating themselves from the same enemy and establishing themselves into a united Africa for the African? Do you think the spirit of unity was created by themselves? No, it is the work of Allah to fulfill all that is written of Him by His prophets that He would do in these last days of the devils' world. (It is in your Bible.) If you are afraid of the truth, then how can truth help you when you disbelieve and are afraid of it? For such, the truth becomes your enemy.

ALLAH HAS revealed the truth of Jesus and His religion - that he was only a prophet (and was not the equal of Moses and Muhammad), and His religion was Islam, and not the Christianity of the Pope of Rome. Allah also revealed that Jesus was sent to the Jews and the Jews rejected him; therefore, hew was unable to lead or convert them to Allah's religion, Islam, and that he died for his failure to accomplish that which he desired to do.

The truth of Jesus' death and burial God has revealed, and has condemned the fancy story of your Bible, of Jesus' rising from death and is somewhere alive sitting on the right hand of His father waiting for the judgement of this world to return to earth again. No one after death has ever gone any place but where they were carried. There is no heaven or hell other than on the earth for you and me, and Jesus was no exception. His body is still embalmed in Palestine and will remain there. Truth has come and false will vanish.

THE WHITE RACE'S FALSE CLAIM TO DIVINITY

7-25-59

THE devil's struggle against us, their power, and authority, is now slipping since the appearance of Allah. Now they have begun to spread false teachings to trap the so-called Negroes. As soon as truth comes to them, they are prepared to try to crush it and keep their 400-year-old slaves dumb. It is actually a race between God and the devil to win the American so-called Negroes. Allah wants to sit the Negroes in heaven and the devil wants to keep them in hell. As it is written of them: "And the serpent (the devil) cast out of his mouth (false) water as a flood after the woman, (the Messenger of Allah and his followers) that he might cause her to be carried away of the flood." (Rev. 12:15). Here, you have that the devils will flood the people with false teachings to try to prevent the progress of the truth. But the falsehood is destined to come to naught, for God has revealed to me the truth - it is the salvation of my people. With it, I will fight the world of Satan and his followers until they submit and are destroyed. With it, I will fight the world of Satan and his followers until they submit and are destroyed. (The white race hates the truth that is now making them manifest for fear of losing the Negroes).

The Lord God of Islam is my defense. He will defend me against my enemies. He loves me and I love Him because I seek to do His will, and He knows that I love my people, whom He loves, and has come to deliver us from the power of the devils, that we may become His servant, and dwell in His presence in peace and security.

THE DEVILS SAY to you that they are better than you and I. Really, they are after the so-called Negroes whom they have crushed, made blind, deaf and dumb. They have robbed and experimented on us for 400 years, and all other darker people whom they have come in contact. Now they stand before you saying, "I am better than you." As he says in the Holy Qur'an: "I am better than he; thou hast created me of fire, while him thou didst create of dust." (7:12)

According to the world of Allah to me, the white race was created in haste. (See Chapter 21:37). Their father, Yakub, was in such a hurry to put his new people on earth as rulers, that he married them while very young (15 and 16 years of age).

Knowing that they had only 6,000 years to go, he rushed them, so says the world of Allah to me. This makes them hasty by nature. They have a fiery temperament; while the original black man is meek and humble. They were made to attract the black people. With this attraction, and other actions of evil and filth, they intended to take you to hell with them. As they say: I will certainly lie in wait for them in Thy straight path; I will certainly come to them from before them and from behind them and from their right hand and from their left hand; and Thou shalt not find most of them thankful. And the devil swore to them both; most-surely, I am a sincere adviser to you." (7:12,16,17,21)

Our father created and made the universe, and one of us made them. As we made the present universe, we will build a new universe. Can the white scientists do the same? We played sleep while they worked; now we are awaking and will build a new world which will make yours look like child's play. We have above you seven inhabited worlds - they are with us These seven worlds or heavens, the stars and the moon show the weight of our brains. what do you have that we did not give you? You shall soon come to know who is the wisest and the most powerful.

INDEX

THANK YOU FOR PURCHASING THIS BOOK.
WE TRUST THE READING WAS REWARDING
AND ENLIGHTENING.

We offer a comprehensive collection of Messenger Elijah Muhammad's works. These works include:

- **Standard Published Titles**
- **Unpublished & Diligently Transcribed Compilations**
- **Audio Cassettes**
- **Video Cassettes**
- **Audio CD's**
- **DVD's**
- **Rare Articles**

You are welcomed to sample a catalog of these items by simply requesting a FREE archive Catalog.

Our contact information is as follows:

Secretarius MEMPS Publications
111 E Dunlap Ave, Ste 1-217
Phoenix, Arizona 85020-7802
Phone & Fax 602 466-7347 ●
Email: secmemps@gmail.com
Web: www.memps.com

Wholesale options are also available.

Made in the USA
Monee, IL
07 July 2026

56552044R00075